Impossible is just
an opinion!

CATCHING
GIANTS

World-beating business lessons from the small team with a big dream that took on the world and won

KEVIN GASKELL

Catching Giants
ISBN 978-1-912300-52-5
eISBN 978-1-912300-53-2

Published in 2022 by SRA Books
Printed in the UK

A CIP record of this book is available from the British Library.

CONTENTS

Thank you

This book is dedicated to everyone who has ever inspired me, shared an idea with me, given me a nudge to get going, or offered me a hand to help when times have been difficult. It is for the dreamers and the doers, for the leaders who encourage others to make a difference and for the people who ultimately make the difference.

It is for the passionate. Those who really care about what they do and the results they deliver. Those who are thoughtful, creative and motivated to dare to dream about what could be possible. By doing so, they inspire others to challenge boundaries and drive progress.

Rowing an ocean and setting a new world record is a privileged experience for the crew. In addition to the rowing crew, success on the water also requires a support team who selflessly give their time and energy. Through these pages I am passing on my thanks to the Ocean5 rowing crew and to the shore team for their dedication and friendship during our incredible voyage. The rowing crew remained positive and enthusiastic, even in the most difficult situations. The shore team never sought to dissuade us from our outrageous objective and continuously provided support wrapped in encouragement. In particular, I would like to thank my daughter Sara who did so much to keep the project visible for our sponsors, without whose generosity we would not have been able to take up the fight against plastics in the oceans.

Finally, I would like to say how grateful I am for the company of everyone who has ever shared a journey with me, whether as a traveller in the wild or as a colleague in business. We have strived together, learned together and grown stronger together. Every journey has been its own adventure and has delivered its own valuable lessons, many of which are shared in this book. Together, we have achieved ambitious goals and proved to ourselves that what we first thought impossible is actually doable.

INTRODUCTION

Impossible is just a big word thrown around by small men who find it easier to live in the world they've been given than to explore the power they have to change it. Impossible is not a fact. It's an opinion. Impossible is not a declaration. It's a dare. Impossible is potential. Impossible is temporary. Impossible is nothing.

– Muhammad Ali

It is common sense that amateur sportsmen or women cannot beat Olympic athletes. Just as it is perceived wisdom that a small business could never beat Microsoft or Volkswagen in a fight to be the best. It's obviously impossible. Or is it?

In a sport such as rowing, the argument is that novice rowers will never beat an Olympic crew for technique and power. They would never be able to compete in a straight-out race for speed. The same argument would tell you that a small, or new, business can never compete with a global brand for market share. It just wouldn't have the budget, skill or experience. But if we changed the sporting comparison to something more complex, where there was scope for innovation and a fresh approach, would the answer be the same? Setting a new world record for rowing across an ocean is about much more than straight-line speed, just as delivering extraordinary results in business is about much more than defeating existing scale and spending power.

Microsoft and Volkswagen were once small businesses. In their early days they succeeded through innovation, drive and by behaving differently to the existing giants. As they grew, they became more powerful and intimidated the market – but they also slowed their rate of innovation. This created opportunities for brave new entrants. Companies such as Google, Netflix, Stripe, Tesla and Venturi were once young, innovative businesses which identified those opportunities and capitalised on them. Now they are the giants themselves and so the cycle repeats with fresh business models such as Arctoris, Monzo Bank, PensionBee, Hopin and Getaround winning in the market.

Asking the question again: can amateurs beat professional athletes and can new businesses beat the existing giants? Given the right conditions, the answer then is yes in both cases. Can you use that information to improve your own sport performance, business performance, project delivery or even your success in life? Again, the answer is yes and this book will show you how to do it. This book explains how a team of amateur sportsmen and businessmen went from never having rowed a boat to becoming world champions in 1,000 days. It will explain how to apply the lessons of that remarkable feat to your own sport, project or business.

This is a story of how an amateur team beat the best and the rest. Not by out-rowing, but by out-thinking, out-planning and out-delivering. By focusing on every area where they could use their abilities to make a difference. By using the skills and techniques from their varied backgrounds to do it differently. By making sure that they challenged every single aspect of the project and set new standards in their preparation and organisation.

Becoming world class required the team to have absolute clarity on the goal that they were setting out to achieve. To deliver that goal they created an inspiring culture of teamwork and honesty, allowing them to complement each other's skills and perform at their best during periods of extreme adversity. They left their egos onshore as they set off to row across the Atlantic Ocean in winter, with the clear goal of setting a new world record for the fastest-ever crossing.

The Atlantic Ocean does not respect anyone's CV or reputation. It treats everyone the same and visitors soon realise they are in the world of the ocean. The ocean sets the rules; it does what it chooses, when it chooses. Crossing the Atlantic Ocean in a tiny rowing boat in winter is a privilege. An opportunity to see and experience situations which most people would never consider. The Talisker Whisky Atlantic Challenge is a chance to pit leadership, physical endurance and organisational skills against the worst that the Atlantic Ocean and mother nature can offer while racing against some of the best rowers in the world.

For any crew to set a new world record for the fastest-ever Atlantic crossing would be a fantastic result. For five guys who had never rowed before to deliver that record would be almost incredible. We were repeatedly told that what we were setting out to do was impossible, but as Muhammad Ali said, 'Impossible is not a fact. It's an opinion. Impossible is not a declaration. It's a dare.'

This is the story of how five ordinary guys achieved something incredible. I was privileged to be a member of that team. This is the account of how we combined our skills to beat the odds – and had fun doing it. I have described how we prepared, how we organised and how we found ways to be more efficient, effective and ultimately successful. I believe that our lessons from this experience are not only suitable for sport and business but can be applied to any challenging environment.

I am sharing the process in the hope that you can adapt it and apply it to your world. Following each chapter is a recap of the business principles which we applied to the Ocean5 project. Each of these principles is offered as a thought starter which I invite you to take and discuss with your colleagues in a 15-minute breakout session. Just let the discussion and ideas flow and remember, don't be afraid to dare to dream. I will be delighted if it helps you to deliver the extraordinary.

Kevin Gaskell

1 A MOMENT OF MADNESS IN MONACO

Your goal should scare you a little and excite you a lot.

– Joe Vitale

I have been a business leader for 30 years. I have led large companies, including brands such as Porsche and BMW, and I have founded and led small companies. Some of those small companies have grown into big ones. I have learned the hard way what it takes to build a great team and how to inspire that team to achieve extraordinary results. Before my business career I played competitive cricket. I represented my country and enjoyed every day I spent on the cricket pitch.

I have always argued that both business and sport are simple but not easy. Given logical objectives – for example, to make a profit or win a match – and a clear set of rules, the team selection should be straightforward, the approach to the game uncomplicated and the score easy to monitor – simple!

Unfortunately, it is never that easy. External factors such as the economy, competitor activity and the state of the pitch affect the operating environment. Then internal factors such as team skills, preparation and communication style affect how the team reacts and performs in that complex environment.

Leadership is the difference

In both of these situations the factor which differentiates the performance of the best from the rest is leadership. This is the ability to inspire other people towards the achievement of a clear goal. The ability to prioritise activity and ensure understanding. Effective leadership leads to the development of a culture which encourages the application of the skills and resources available in the way that most efficiently delivers the goal.

Leadership does not need ego. It does need an environment where trust, honesty and transparency are fostered and respected. It needs open communication and the liberal use of praise and expressed gratitude. This breeds confidence and confident teams will strive for improvement and implement innovation. They will trust the organisation to support them, even if a specific innovation delivers disappointing results. Confidence, trust and innovation are the key elements of making progress.

An organisation with a clarity of objective and a culture of confidence, trust and innovation is one where excellence of performance can be described as simple, and easy. In a simple and easy organisation everyone knows what the goal is, what the plan is to achieve the goal and how they contribute to the plan. I have spent my career striving to build organisations which operate in this way.

Outside the office I relax by taking myself off to remote parts of the world. I have walked, with my son, to both the North and South Poles and together we have climbed some of the world's highest mountains. As well as acting as a welcome distraction from the demands of leading companies, these expeditions allow me to develop my thoughts on leadership. I am fortunate to have been a member of expedition teams guided by excellent leaders. Trust, honesty and transparency need to be taken to a whole new level when you are hanging off a rope 3,000 metres up a mountain and you ask your climbing partner whether the safety line is secure. There is only one version of the truth, and the answer has to be either yes or no. 'I don't know' is not an acceptable reply, nor is 'I think so', nor is delegating the responsibility for the answer to someone else!

Speaking from experience

I am privileged to be invited to speak to audiences all over the world about leadership, teamwork and how I believe it is possible for ordinary people (of which I proudly consider myself one) to build great companies and extraordinary teams.

In my talks I use examples from companies I have led to explain my approach to leadership. I share photographs and explain situations from my expeditions to illustrate points on organisation, teamwork and accountability. Examples such as the safety line question demonstrate that the soft elements of leadership – trust, honesty and integrity – have real, hard consequences. This allows me to explain why I believe that inspirational leadership requires a blend of soft skills and hard facts.

Taken together these factors build an inspirational culture where the team feels valued and responsible. With absolute clarity on what success looks like, authority must be shared and permission given to the team to make the decisions on how best to achieve the goals. This is a fundamental building block in the development of accountability, which in turn leads to the achievement of extraordinary results.[1]

---

1 See Gaskell, K. (2017). *Inspired Leadership*. Wiley.

One November evening I had spoken at the Monaco Yacht Club, Monte Carlo, to around 300 local business leaders and entrepreneurs. I had covered the topic of leadership development and shared my belief that effective leadership is the biggest single factor in the long-term success, or otherwise, of any team or organisation. The audience were young leaders from the marine sector and after my talk they had been enthusiastically questioning me on ways to best develop their own leadership skills.

As I prepared to leave the podium, I was asked one final question: 'What have you planned for your next expedition?' It was an interesting question to which I didn't have a ready answer. I had only recently returned to Europe after my son Matt and I had climbed Carstensz Pyramid in Papua, Indonesia. The mountain is one of the '7 summits', the name given to the group of the highest mountains on each of the Earth's seven continents. It had been a challenging expedition from which I was still recovering and I hadn't started to consider what my next adventure should be.

In a matter of moments, I reflected on a chat I had with Peter van Kets[2] a few months previously. Peter is a professional endurance adventurer and a good friend of mine who was telling me about his experiences of rowing across the Atlantic Ocean. He took great delight in sharing the gory details of the pain, suffering and terror he went through during his 76 days at sea. He finished his story with the words, 'Kev, you should do it – you would love it!'

I dismissed Peter's outrageous suggestion immediately and hadn't given it more than a few moments' thought since. But here I was speaking to a marine audience and on the spot to answer the question. So, I replied, 'Well, I have thought about rowing across the Atlantic, and since you ladies and gentlemen

---

2 See https://petervankets.co.za

are involved in the marine industry, would anybody like to come with me?' The response was some nervous laughter and a few comments suggesting that I was crazy.

Get yourself committed

The talk ended, and drinks and canapes were served. It is always fun to meet the audience and continue the discussion. The guy who had asked the question about my next adventure walked over and joined the group. He then asked whether I was serious about the Atlantic row. Not wishing to backtrack in front of him or other members of the audience, I replied that I was but I had a few small shortcomings – I had never rowed a boat, I had never sailed a boat, I didn't know anything about the sea and I had no idea how to navigate. Other than those tiny challenges, I was good to go.

I expected him to give me a polite, humorous response and then we would both drop the whole crazy idea. Instead, he explained that he worked as a superyacht crewman and had a working knowledge of the sea. He also explained that he had two friends and that they would all like to join my team for the Atlantic row. What team? What row? I didn't know the first thing about it. Until five minutes ago I hadn't seriously considered doing such a thing. But I wasn't about to disappoint everybody by immediately backing out.

We agreed that he and I, together with his keen friends, would meet up in the UK and we would talk seriously about what it would take to enter a boat in the Talisker Whisky Atlantic Challenge. That was my first meeting with Will Hollingshead and he was deadly serious about entering the race.

The seed was sown. In a moment of madness, I had made a public commitment, in front of 300 witnesses, and now there was no turning back.

1: NOTES FOR BUSINESS

Ordinary people can and do achieve extraordinary success. If you want to achieve something special, you have to aim high because behind every example of success prowls a dream. This is the dream which leaders use to inspire their teams to build something new, to create something special. Delivering this dream is the definition of the vision of success. This vision must be authentic, inspirational and aspirational. Clear communication is needed to enable the translation of the dream into a practical plan and encourage the team to pursue stretching goals.

Leaders imagine the point where success has been delivered and work back from there to where they are currently. By considering the entire journey, the priorities and actions necessary to progress towards success can be defined. This way dreams are translated into practical plans and the journey begins. The journey is divided into achievable stages so that the excitement of achieving the goals at each stage generates the energy and passion for the next steps.

Leaders who achieve the most aspirational goals recognise the scale of the challenge while also firmly believing that the vision of success is achievable. They support their teams with positive recognition of the progress they make. They encourage others to demonstrate creativity and maintain courage when fear creeps in. Successful leaders invite their team on a shared journey where pride, passion and inspiration are embedded into the culture that they develop.

Do you have a clear goal? What does extraordinary success look like for you?
Your vision of where you want to go or who you want to be is the greatest asset that you have. Without having a goal, it is impossible to score. Do not use numbers to set a limit on your imagination. If you want to achieve long-term success then be brave and demand excellence of yourself. Describe what extraordinary success looks like and enthusiastically share that vision.

Do you want to be good at your job, or do you want to be a leader?
Many people settle for being mediocre. They do enough to perform the tasks expected of them. What are you going to do that sets you apart from the others? Leaders have ambition and demand more of themselves. The most successful leaders strive for world class.

What are you prepared to invest?
To be truly exceptional demands commitment, and commitment demands time. Leaders understand that they must invest time and effort to develop themselves and their skills. Leaders are not afraid of criticism. Leaders grow through experiences, both good and painful.

Leadership is the difference
Leadership is the ability to inspire other people to move the organisation towards the achievement of a clear shared goal. The ability to prioritise activity and to ensure understanding is what achieves results. For this to be possible the leaders must first have clarity on the goals of the organisation and be able to share the excitement of the challenge.

Leadership does not need ego
Leaders build cultures where trust, honesty and transparency are fostered and respected. Leaders use open communication. They recognise that their praise and expressed gratitude will develop confident teams. Leaders delegate opportunities and trust and they pass the credit to the team for progress made.

Clarity, priority, focus
Absolute clarity on the vision of success and an unconditional focus on delivering the priority actions for that success is what separates the successful leaders from the rest.

2 CHOOSE YOUR TEAM AS IF YOUR LIFE DEPENDS UPON IT

**A team is not a group of people who work together.
A team is a group of people who trust each other.**

– Simon Sinek

Having looked into the details of the race and discussed it with my son Matt, I started to get excited about what this challenge could be. While Matt and I have completed several expeditions together, they have all been on land or ice, and we knew nothing about rowing, boats or the preparation needed to cross an ocean.

Decide to decide

We met our prospective crewmates at the Cotswold Water Park Hotel a few weeks later. Will Hollingshead arrived with his friends Chris Hodgson and Sam Coxon. They were all experienced superyacht crew and had far more marine knowledge and experience than either Matt or me. My first impression was that they were a really good bunch of guys. Friendly, bright, smart and keen to discuss the race. They were intrigued by the idea of rowing across an ocean that they had previously crossed in a 50-metre superyacht. This potential crossing would be very different.

My second impression was that their enthusiasm, while contagious, was bordering on naivety. They were very clear that they wanted to go as soon as possible and to set a new world record! I knew from previous experience that to put a project like this together would take lengthy and meticulous planning. The training and preparation would be a huge commitment and the idea of setting a new world record seemed ludicrous.

Despite my misgivings, we each recognised what the other group would bring to the party. Will, Chris and Sam would bring youth, strength, marine knowledge and experience of weeks at sea. Matt and I would bring planning skills, endurance and experience of performing in hostile environments.

Regarding their enthusiasm for setting a new world record, I felt that since I was twice their age, and none of us had rowed, it was highly unlikely that we would come anywhere near the existing record.

I suggested they consider doing the crossing once with me in the boat. They could then replace me with a hyper-fit 30-year-old and go again, this time for the record, applying all of the lessons from the first crossing. The discussions were fun and exciting. We agreed to go away and each reflect on what we were potentially intending to do. We would meet again in two weeks to decide whether to register an entry for the race.

Accept the challenge

It was clear when we met again that everyone was excited about the race. We had studied the details of the row and understood the inherent dangers involved in attempting such a crossing. Rather than being scared off by our research, we had become more enthusiastic. But we still needed to specifically define the challenge. We needed to be clear about what it was we were setting out to achieve.

The scale of the task was pretty daunting. It was to row, in the winter, from La Gomera in the Canary Islands, Spain to English Harbour, Antigua, in the Caribbean. That was a distance of over 3,000 miles across 100 million square miles of Atlantic Ocean, facing anything and everything that the sea and weather could throw at us. It meant spending up to 55 days in a tiny plastic rowing boat, carrying everything we would need. We would row in shifts for 24 hours per day, every day. Sleep would be minimal. We would have no shelter from the weather, no comforts and no rescue if anything went seriously wrong.

We would have to be able to contribute, work and live together in an extreme situation for 24 hours a day every day. There would be absolutely nowhere to hide. Extreme hardship would quickly uncover negative traits – or, if we chose our crewmates carefully, would amplify the positive spirit within the team.

The whole must be greater than the sum of its parts

We each brought a different perspective to the challenge. Will, Chris and Sam understood the scale of an ocean crossing because they had done it before – but in a big boat. Those crossings were in style and luxury with comfortable beds, showers, TV, chef and a big engine! This time it would be very, very different.

It was clear that they had determination, intelligence and marine experience and were good together. They had an obvious sense of humour and were used to working hard for long hours as superyacht crew.

Matt and I had a lot of experience of pulling an expedition together and then delivering it. We understood that something like an ocean crossing was going to take at least two years to plan, organise, train for and deliver. We were quieter than the other guys but no less determined and enthusiastic. It became clear that if we combined their skills and personality with Matt's and mine, we would have a team with a balance of attributes which could make a very competent crew – albeit that none of us had ever rowed anywhere!

For the next few hours, we discussed the project in detail. We shared our ambitions and hopes, our fears and concerns. Every potential team member interviewed each of the others. We were choosing our team as if our lives depended on it – because it very well may! We recognised that we could work well together, that our skills would complement and combine and, critically, that we liked each other. The decision was made – we were going to enter the race.

And the youngsters were still talking about setting a new world record.

A team is formed

We had a team. We had looked each other in the eyes and confirmed that we could work together, have fun together, and we aimed to row an ocean together. Our team was five guys with different backgrounds. Here's how we described ourselves in our marketing material:

Sam Coxon – Employed in the superyacht industry until he realised his natural ability as an endurance athlete by winning a gold medal at a national triathlon event. With a passion for ultra-endurance competitions, Sam has created his own fitness and training business and in 2017 was selected to represent Great Britain in the triathlon world championship.

Kevin Gaskell – A business leader and serial entrepreneur, Kevin has led a number of major companies. He has walked to both the North Pole and to the South Pole as well as climbing some of the world's highest mountains. He brings a mature aspect to the team and is vastly experienced at leading complex projects and demanding expeditions.

Matt Gaskell – With a degree in conservation biology and another in medicine, Matt will be the crew's medic. He has also walked to both the North and South Poles and climbed some of the world's highest mountains. A keen triathlete and endurance swimmer, Matt was selected to carry the 2012 Olympic torch. He has quiet patience, which is key to interpreting the rules and regulations of the race.

Chris Hodgson – Having spent much of his childhood playing in the waters of Pembrokeshire, Chris is no stranger to the sea. As a senior officer on board superyachts, Chris has travelled all over the globe and completed three Atlantic crossings. He is a highly competent leader able to achieve results quietly but firmly. With proven nautical experience and a passion for extreme sports, his endurance and practical skills are a key component of the team's approach.

Will Hollingshead – After five years working in the superyacht industry, Will moved into marina management. An entrepreneur at heart, he is the co-founder of an ocean security business. Full of ideas and energy, Will can always be found trying something new and different. An experienced water sports instructor, Will is as strong as an ox, an attribute expected to be useful in a rowing boat at sea.

The Ocean5 project is born

To complete our entry documentation, we needed a team name and a designated skipper. Since we were five guys aiming to row across an ocean, we called ourselves The Ocean5 – simple, straightforward and it does what it says on the tin!

It was equally simple to elect our skipper. Chris was, by far, the most experienced mariner and a serving superyacht officer. He is also a top bloke and has an excellent way with people. Unanimous decision made.

Journal, April 22nd 2018

Exciting day. Looks like we have a team for the Atlantic row. Have now met Will, Chris and Sam a few times and they are really good guys – and keen sportsmen so they're fit! They all have marine experience, which is great, but no expedition experience, which is not unusual. I think that this crossing will be a shock for them, but I think it will be a shock for me and Matt as well...

While we were not yet rowers, we did each have a connection with the sea – whether as sailors, endurance swimmers, triathletes or scuba divers. That connection fed our passion for the health of the world's oceans. We agreed that we should use this project to raise awareness of the fight against plastics in the seas. We carefully researched organisations which would support this cause. After careful consideration, we selected the Plastic Soup Foundation.[3] We were attracted to their focus

---

3 See https://www.plasticsoupfoundation.org

on programmes demonstrating the effect of ocean plastics on marine and human health. They have exposed where the problems lie, both within industry and the government, and have led successful campaigns to reduce microplastics and plastic pollution. We especially liked their focus on educational activities as one of the most important ways to reduce plastic waste. With an understanding of the damage that is being done, their belief is that these children will grow to be the positive influencers of the future. We were proud to recognise their work as our cause and set ourselves the target of raising US$250,000 to support their programmes.

The Ocean5 project was launched. Now all we had to do was to put the project together, get a boat, learn how to row, pass all of the stipulated Royal Yachting Association (RYA) training programmes, learn extreme survival skills, get qualified in first aid (and second aid – taking care of others!), get ourselves fit enough to row an ocean, raise $250,000, get to the start line – and not forget to have fun!

Four millennials and a boomer in a boat – and the millennials intended to set a new world record! What could possibly go wrong?

2: NOTES FOR BUSINESS

Trust is critical within any successful team. It is built through clarity, honesty and openness. It is reinforced by team members sharing a set of values and agreed operating standards. Shared values are an essential part of creating a team culture which will withstand the most difficult situations. The values will determine the way that communication develops in the organisation and the way that members of the team relate to each other. Clarity of objective and a set of shared values will support honest communication and ensure discussions are focused on the achievement of the goals.

Uncertainty and adversity will reveal the strength of the organisation's character. For leaders, the toughest times provide the most severe test of their credentials and of their responsibility towards those in their care.

The most capable leaders will continue to apply the shared values and will achieve challenging goals by the development and recognition of more leaders. This means identifying natural leaders at every level in the organisation and inspiring them to accept ownership of challenges then trusting them to engage their team in the positive delivery of results.

The most capable leaders recognise their own limitations. They combine their skills with colleagues and team members to form a unit which is stronger than the sum of the capabilities of its members. The best leaders delegate clearly and provide the authority and accountability for the team members to deliver the goal. Open communication at all times reinforces trust.

Organisational values must be visible

Shared values must be openly discussed, clearly visible and applied consistently to the business operation. Properly communicated shared values will strengthen the business culture and create a sense of unity within the team. Regular application of shared values will inspire engagement and create stronger bonds within the organisation.

Ensure the team have a shared ambition

Everyone in the organisation should be fully aware of the vision of success and what it means. This should not be a set of financial targets but a carefully considered definition of what the organisation will be like when it is successful. Leadership is responsible for ensuring that there is a clear understanding of the goals and a determination within the team to achieve that success. There is no room in the team for individuals who do not aspire to the same goals.

Combine skills to create superteams

Every individual has a different mix of skills and talents. Carefully select team members to bring their specific combination of skills to the achievement of the team goal. With clear delegation of authority and clarity of purpose, the team performance will exceed the sum of its individual contributors. If necessary, periodically rebalance team membership with the positive message of applying extracted skills elsewhere.

Develop trust in times of adversity

A great culture is of no value if the team don't trust the leaders or each other. Always be truthful and communicate fully, especially when news is not positive or times are difficult. When success is achieved, make the team feel special and their performance recognised by celebrating loudly and visibly. If a project is struggling, make that an opportunity to build trust by making sure that team members do not feel exposed or caught out. Always use problems as positive learning opportunities.

Hire for attitude, train for skill

Build your organisation around people who demonstrate the ability to operate positively and effectively as part of a team. Look for people who radiate upbeat confidence and constructive energy. Actively seek such people and be prepared to invest in the skill training necessary for them to be successful in the role you have defined.

Don't be a genius – build a genius team

Recognise that people have different experiences and alternative ways of approaching a challenge. Apparently, everyone is at least five per cent genius. A leader's role is to align the team so that they can focus their blended skills on the delivery of a shared goal. Combining the five per cent genius of 20 individuals on a specific goal creates the equivalent of a complete genius.

3 DARE TO DREAM

Only those who will risk going too far can possibly find out how far one can go.

– T.S. Eliot

After many years of interviewing potential new team members and supporting friends and colleagues to achieve their full potential, it is my belief that the majority of people never really consider what they want to achieve in life. They follow the path suggested by the opportunities and challenges which pop up in front of them. I am firmly of the view that if you don't set out to build your own vision of success, then you will spend your life helping other people to build theirs.

We all have the same number of hours in a week as Leonardo da Vinci, Einstein, Mother Theresa or Martin Luther King Jr. Each of these extraordinary people left a legacy for mankind. Success doesn't have to be measured in scientific advances or humanitarian progress, or even in monetary terms. An individual's success can be measured as movement towards the goal that they set for themselves. People who achieve their dream do so because they define it clearly, objectively and openly. They can then prioritise and apply the hours they have been given to the enjoyment of pursuing that goal. Delivering something that once seemed impossible is just great fun.

Define your vision of success

What was to be the goal for the row? To get across safely and to have fun was a good starting point for a successful row. To raise $250,000 for the Plastic Soup Foundation to help to protect the ocean would be another significant measure of success, but the young guys in the crew were clear that setting a new world record was going to be their ultimate measure of success. By its very definition, that required us to become a world-class team – and we had to achieve that in a space of time that would normally be considered impossible.

World-class athletes begin their journey as children; world-class teams select the very best athletes and train together for years. We had 1,000 days – less than three years – to take five guys who had never rowed and turn them into a world-class unit. This meant that we had to employ effort over natural ability. That meant our endurance, skills, preparation, processes and mentality had to be world class by the time we arrived at the start line. Each of us had a personal responsibility to be completely prepared and competent in survival, navigation, seamanship, radio communication and, above all, fitness. There was no room for ego because there would be nowhere to hide when the race started.

To become world class

Every team entering the race will ask themselves what a decent performance looks like. Some would be aiming to win the race and would ask themselves, 'What does a great performance look like?' We were asking, 'What is world class?'

In every competitive or skills-based activity, someone somewhere is considered to be world class. We wanted to find them, learn from them, exceed them. We had to ask ourselves what we were prepared to invest in terms of time and effort, and what other activities we were prepared to give up to be able to dedicate sufficient time to this project. We defined world class as beating the world record for the fastest unsupported five-man row from east to west across the Atlantic. It was a ridiculous goal because we were rowing novices – naive, ignorant, just plain stupid. Worse, we feared that if we spoke about our goal too openly, we would be considered arrogant. But records are there to be broken and if somebody was going to break the record, why should it not be us?

Now we had something to shoot at. If you don't shoot at a clearly defined goal, you are never going to hit it. With a clear goal we could work together to create a 1,000-day plan to success. We would be learning as we went, there would be difficulties and we would make mistakes along the way, but we would use those challenges to increase our knowledge and strength. We considered how we would present ourselves and decided that at all stages we needed to look like and behave like a world-class team.

This would support our aim to build the performance culture we needed and to send a message to the world, including potential sponsors, that we were a seriously competitive and properly organised team. Photographs of a team smartly presented in team kit increase the power of social media marketing. Each time a crew member arrived at a meeting on time, dressed in team kit and fully prepared increased the chances of a potential sponsor or interested journalist taking a positive decision to support The Ocean5.

Develop collective confidence

Looking and sounding like a team breeds a feeling of camaraderie and belief. We knew that we would face huge challenges even to get to the race start line. Building belief in each other and the project would be a critical part of achieving success.

Displaying confidence is an essential behaviour in the successful pursuit of any goal. It encourages individuals to become self-reliant, committed, resilient and focused. What we were setting out to achieve (even without the world record ambition) was challenging and scary. Crossing the Atlantic Ocean in a small open rowing boat is a daunting thought at any time. In difficult situations, a lack of confidence can cause individuals to doubt themselves, act irrationally, or even in extreme situations to give up. Due to the huge amount of personal preparation and training that was needed, we could not afford the risk of anyone giving up before the race start. We absolutely could not afford anyone to give up during the race because they would then become a liability and 150 kg of body and kit that the other rowers would have to carry. We knew of it happening in previous crossings when rowers had become paralysed with fear.

We had decided how we would display our confidence externally. We would present in team kit, we would speak with knowledge and passion, we would always behave like a world-class team. Our level of internal confidence, though, was probably even more important. Internal confidence is not easily seen, but under difficult situations it shows as encouragement or unprompted help given by one crew member to another. Self-confidence means crew members are aware of their positive impact on the total team activity and an understanding of how they can help to fill gaps or support dips in the performance of the team immediately but informally. Internal confidence allows us to know who we are, what our strengths are and what we are capable of doing, even in the most difficult situations.

If we were going to perform to a world-class level, it would need each of us to support each other through the challenging periods that we knew we would face. Only by each of us being confident in ourselves and in the team as a whole would we be strong enough to perform at 100 per cent.

Bring the plan to life

Had we overestimated what we could possibly achieve? Were we pushing for a goal too far? Probably. But we were convinced that with an explicit clarity of intention, total dedication to the project, absolute attention to detail and the physical delivery of everything we possibly could during the race, we might, just might, be able to achieve something extraordinary. As Malcolm Gladwell writes in his book *David and Goliath* '... the fact of being an underdog can change people... it can open doors and create opportunities and educate and enlighten and make possible what might otherwise have seemed unthinkable.'[4] Now we had to educate and enlighten ourselves. We would bring the dream to life and create a plan which made our ambitions tangible, visible and deliverable. Then we would find a way to make them achievable.

Understand the challenge

We needed to break down the challenge into its component parts. Then we could start to build our plan for how we would approach each part. It was important to see how the race was organised and how other crews prepared themselves and their boats for the crossing.

---

4 Gladwell, M. (2013). *David and Goliath*. Penguin.

Chris, Sam and I agreed to travel to La Gomera to investigate the preparations for the race that would take place one year before we were due to start. We would make sure that we were familiar with the event and the organisation. As well as taking the mystery out of the start venue, the support available and pre-race accommodation offered, we would look for examples of best practice. Other crews would have ideas and processes which we hadn't yet thought of and which we would be able to use to improve our own planning and preparation. We wanted to research all parts of the race and the preparation. We intended to speak to the Atlantic Campaigns organising team and the rowing crews as well as checking out local chandleries, suppliers and general facilities.

La Gomera is not the easiest place to get to and all of this had to be done over a long weekend, so we would record our observations with notes, photographs and videos of everything interesting that we saw. We could prioritise the information once we were back with our full team in the UK.

A long weekend in Spain

Travelling from a wet and cold UK to the balmy climate of La Gomera in December wasn't too much of a hardship. After a full day of cars, planes and ferries we arrived in the Puerto De San Sebastián de La Gomera. It is a thriving port with major ferry links and commercial traffic to Tenerife and beyond.

We were immediately struck by what a big deal the race is to the people and visitors of the island. All around the port were flags, banners and billboards announcing the start of the race. Around the marina were the various race control offices, the crew meeting marquee and the central car park, which had been converted into a boat preparation area. Even though it was late in the evening, many of the crews were still busily working on their boats. After a very long day of travelling, we headed for our hotel to get some sleep before starting a busy weekend of fact-finding.

The following morning, over an early breakfast in the town plaza, we agreed on our approach. We would first head to the boat park to register as official guests and then meet the crews who were still preparing their boats on dry land, then attend a briefing arranged by the organisers before heading down to the marina to meet the teams whose boats had already been launched into the water. That would take us the whole day, after which we would head to the Blue Marlin bar where each evening many of the rowers congregated to share their thoughts over a meal and a beer.

After registering with the organisers, Atlantic Campaigns, we were each issued with a lanyard saying 'Next Year's Rower' which gave us access to all areas. It was five days before the scheduled start of the race and remarkable to see the different levels of preparedness of the crews in the boat park. Most were well advanced and just waiting for the lift into the water but a number appeared to be well behind the schedule with urgent crews busily working on different aspects of packing, checking, fixing, fettling, stickering and a hundred other jobs. The amount of food and kit to be packed into the boats was incredible. It simply didn't look as if there was room for everything. We spoke to the crews, who were generous with their limited time, and asked them for their best tips on how to be ready to take on the Atlantic. Start the preparation earlier was the most frequent reply!

By contrast, the crews of the boats already in the marina were far more relaxed. They had packed their boats and were spending their time checking and rechecking and taking a leisurely row around the bay beyond the marina. This allowed them to test their water maker (for drinking water), autohelm, radio and navigation equipment while working off some of their excess nervous energy. Again, we talked to many of the crews and picked up a host of ideas, actions and tips for effective preparation. One of the most frequent pieces of advice was that if you think you are going to need it (whatever it is), make sure you bring it with you from the UK. Any piece of equipment that was missing or broken would probably (maybe!) only be available in Tenerife and that was a one-hour ferry trip away – and the ferry only ran every four hours. It was becoming clearer that the planning was a critical element of a successful campaign.

One crew in particular stood out from all of the others because of their calmness and serenity. The Dutch Atlantic Four[5] were a four-man Dutch team who were never going to win first prize in the creative name competition, but everything about them and their boat was absolutely world class. When we introduced ourselves and asked how they were, their reply was 'bored'! That was not necessarily the response we expected and so we enquired further.

The race regulations stipulated that all crews must be in La Gomera for a minimum of ten days before the race begins. This is to allow for any last-minute problems or oversights to be dealt with before the boat is submitted for final scrutineering immediately before it is lowered into water. In truth it is also an opportunity for the less well-prepared crews to get themselves organised, complete the final preparation tasks and pass scrutineering.

They explained that they were experienced ocean rowers who had competed in open water races all over Europe. They had done all of their preparation and thought about every little detail long before their boat was transported to La Gomera. They proudly showed us around their boat explaining each of the innovations, modifications and operational improvements that they had built into her. They spoke about teamwork and

---

5 See https://dutchatlanticfour.com

how they challenged and motivated each other rather than allowing any one person's ego to become a problem. They were a great crew – humble, focused and organised – but were feeling a bit bored because they were ready to go and it was still another five days before the race started. It was clear to us that the Dutch Atlantic Four already had a head start in the race – and the race hadn't started yet.

They were incredibly generous in sharing their advice and information as we took notes and photographs of their ideas and innovations. They were delighted when we explained that we had the clear intention of using their wisdom and experience to improve our own chances. They recognised that we weren't racing against them – which was good for us because they went on to achieve a decisive overall win in their race.

Own the plan

We left La Gomera with a much clearer understanding of the pre-race organisation and what we would need to do to make sure we were competitive even before we started racing. We had ideas from the Dutch Atlantic Four about how we could improve our boat and ourselves. We recognised that the best teams made it look easy. This was because they were so well prepared and had done everything they possibly could do to improve their performance long before they got anywhere near the start line. We confirmed to ourselves what we had already suspected, that planning, preparation and team culture were critical aspects of delivering a successful result.

Journal, December 7th 2018

In La Gomera to do a recce. Impressed by the organisation and the briefing given by Atlantic Campaigns. Crews all look very serious and busy prepping their boats. Met a Dutch team who really have it all organised. Good guys – fully prepared and ready to go 5 days before the start – that's how it should be done. Feels all very real now – seems strange, and scary, that this time next year we will be preparing for the start.

Taking those lessons on board, we carefully built our 1,000-day plan for success and divided it into actionable steps with a designated crew member responsible for each section. Playing to our strengths and natural skills, Sam would organise our fitness and training programme, Matt took on race administration, boat equipment, training course attendance, food supplies and medical support, Will organised sea-based training and harbour authority liaison, Chris was responsible for navigation support and weather routing support and systems, while I would manage boat preparation and marketing.

I always find that translating the shared spoken ambition into a series of practical tasks is fun because that's when it becomes real. Building the 1,000-day plan forced us to consider the project in steps, some of which could operate in parallel, while others were on a critical path and had to be performed to a strict timetable. We used Trello, which is an online productivity and workflow tool, to build our master plan and make sure that, even when the crew weren't physically together, we could still work in a coordinated manner.

We needed to start with basics: read and understand the rules, investigate where we could get a boat from and research the existing world records. Behind those initial data points there was a whole variety of work to complete before we got anywhere near rowing a boat. We needed to find as much information as possible about other rowers, equipment suppliers, boat builders, advisors, weather routers, training availability and timetable, existing world records, potential sponsors, press relationships and so forth. Our list stretched to over 300 activities which needed to be completed before we started the race.

While it looked like a daunting list of necessary actions, it acted as a confidence booster. Breaking the project down into smaller pieces and setting realistic goals for each of the actions showed us that we could do this. Against the plan we could move forward step by step and demonstrate visible progress every day. This shared visibility allowed us to prioritise our preparation. We needed to be effective, efficient and organised. If we followed the plan we would be in good shape when we got to the start line.

We had dared to dream about setting a new world record. We had seen how the best teams operate and we had confirmed to ourselves that even if we could not out-row, we could and would out-plan many of our competitors. With our 1,000-day plan we had established our route to turn our dream into something real. While there was now a huge amount of work to do, it felt good to have a tangible plan and to be starting to make progress. We were now converting our passion into action.

3: NOTES FOR BUSINESS

To achieve what most people consider to be unachievable you need to aim beyond what you believe you are capable of. You must change your mindset to develop a complete disregard for where you previously thought your abilities ended. It is not about reflecting on how good you are, but rather about considering how good you want to be and then creating a structured plan to get there.

Many people would call this overstretching. But that's because most people are more concerned with protecting what they have than taking the risks necessary to achieve something truly extraordinary and exciting. Achieving a properly defined vision of success is rarely easy. Most people are afraid of failure and never pause to consider that failure is a necessary step on the path to success. If we don't make a mistake, we aren't pushing far enough or fast enough towards the goal.

The clarity of the goal is critical. It must be objective and defined and in three dimensions. Ask the questions: when my goal is achieved, what will I see? What will I hear? How will I feel? Once a clearly defined goal has been described in a way that is tangible, visible and considered deliverable, a plan can be developed and actions prioritised to deliver that result. Working towards a specific goal with a carefully considered activity plan builds confidence. Confidence is contagious and can be used as energy to drive progress.

Commit to your vision of success
Do not be stalled by fear or delayed by inaction. Make a real commitment to achieving the success that you have defined. Dare to dream – change your limits, change your thinking. Somebody, or some organisation, is the best in the world at everything. Why should it not be you or your organisation?

Find examples of world class
In every business, competitive sport or skills-based activity there are world-class performers. Identify who they are, analyse them

and seek to understand why they are better than their competitors. Examine what you can learn from them and what lessons you can learn from observing areas of their operation which could be applicable to the achievement of your goal.

Connect all activities with a clear plan

A dream without a plan is just a dream. Define the stages to achieving the goal. Break the stages down into smaller projects with defined deliverables. Include members of the team in the discussion. If you don't have a team, invite interested business partners or advisors to join the discussion. By involving others, you will get the benefit of their experience and a broader appreciation of the opportunity and challenge.

Make your vision of success visible – speak about it openly

By making the goal visible you are inviting engagement and inclusion. Encourage discussion of the goal with your team, with suppliers and with clients. Understanding what your vision of success means to them will allow you to refine and adapt the goal to achieve maximum positive benefit. Encourage challenge, creativity and innovation.

Be disciplined

Be organised and structured in translating the plan into action. If you are not, the process will fall into disrepute and recovery will be more difficult than building the plan in the first place. Execution of the plan is not an addition to anyone's job – it *is* their job.

Remain confident

Becoming a world-class operator is challenging. Expect there to be difficult times, but when they arrive maintain a positive mindset. Looking and sounding confident builds belief. It encourages teams to become resilient, committed and focused. If building a world-class organisation was easy, everybody would do it.

4 NOTHING COMES EASY

An organisation's ability to learn, and convert that learning into action rapidly, is the ultimate competitive advantage.

– Jack Welch

The Talisker Whisky Atlantic Challenge, as the row is officially titled, crosses 100 million square miles of Atlantic Ocean. The shortest possible route between San Sebastián de La Gomera and English Harbour, Antigua and Barbuda, is 2,700 nautical miles, which is equivalent to 3,100 land miles. The weather is completely unpredictable and at times we expected to be battling with winds and currents so powerful that we would not be able to row against them. We would be facing waves and swells with heights of up to ten metres – which may not sound too much until you realise we would be sitting in an open eight-metre plastic boat with our backsides less than half a metre above the waterline!

The world record for the five-man crossing was just under 37 days; we knew that we needed to be prepared to row two hours on, two hours off, for 24 hours each day for 50 days or more. Throughout all of that time we needed to navigate, communicate with the maritime authorities, report to race control, dodge big ships, eat, sleep and survive. It is called the world's toughest row for good reason.

Get physical – there's nowhere to hide

We knew that racing across the Atlantic was not for the faint of heart, nor for the faint of body. We also knew that we had to prepare thoroughly. In order to be successful in this harsh environment, each of us needed to maintain a positive mindset. Maintaining positivity becomes much more difficult when your body is suffering acute pain and continuous discomfort under the sheer physical assault of the conditions that we would face at sea in a small rowing boat.

The race would be a huge test of physical endurance. Each rower would be burning 7,000 calories per day. My experience from previous ultra-endurance expeditions was that it is not possible to replace that many calories every day. This was especially true when each of us would be rowing for two hours on, two hours off and needed to find time for sleep, personal hygiene and all boat maintenance and housekeeping tasks. There was simply no rest period long enough to prepare and consume that quantity of food – and in any case our boat weight budget dictated that we could not carry that quantity of food. We needed to plan for a deficiency in the calories our bodies would burn.

Recognising that we were not Olympians and accepting that there would be rowers in the race with greater athletic ability and strength than we had, our approach was going to be effort over ability. Time was tight, so we had to prepare as efficiently and thoroughly as possible. We had individual responsibility to get ourselves into the best physical condition possible. Given our full-time jobs, separate locations and, for Chris and Will, the fact that they were typically working at sea for many months of the year, we had to be flexible in how to build physical training into our regular routines. There could be no excuses; the training just had to be done.

Build on strong foundations

To establish individual endurance and resilience we needed to ensure we each had a strong cardiovascular and muscular foundation. Even before considering the race, we had all trained regularly, so our fitness levels were above average. Now we now needed to move to a completely different level. Sam, a professional personal trainer and member of the GB triathlon squad, developed an escalating training plan for the period up to the race. Accountability for following the plan and logging compliance with the weekly targets was our own individual responsibility. There were no shortcuts. Weekly results were collated by Sam and results displayed on the team website. No excuses for not training were ever requested and none were ever given.

Fitting training between all our other responsibilities and commitments meant that exercise was taken wherever and whenever possible. Will sent a video of himself exercising on a static rower at Shirley Heights overlooking the race finish line at English Harbour, Antigua. Chris posted a video of himself training in the boiling hot engine room of a superyacht. For the rest of us it was less glamorous, with hours spent in gyms, on bikes or running around the countryside. The training plan supplied by Sam was considered a minimum. On every business trip I made I aimed to stay only at hotels with a fitness centre. Being first into the gym or pool in the morning became normal. When at home I enjoyed hiking through the countryside with my polar training rig of a body harness dragging three car tyres.

In the 450 days leading up to the race, the team rowed

4,934 km on a Concept 2 static rower, ran 4,765 km, cycled 9,460 km and lifted 2,248,938 kg of weights (equivalent to the weight of a Royal Navy frigate). In addition, we swam, hiked and collectively spent hundreds of hours during days and nights rowing our boat around the waters off the south coast of England. We were determined that a lack of physical fitness was not going to be the limiting factor on our record attempt.

Rules are *not* meant to be broken

Compliance with a set of rules for a race is not normally front of mind two years before the race starts. But this race was of a different scale. The Talisker Whisky Atlantic Challenge is owned and organised by Atlantic Campaigns, a company which specialises in promoting and managing ocean rowing races. They have long experience, and the core team of Carsten Heron Olsen, Nikki Holter and Ian Couch, in addition to being a pleasure to work with, are highly knowledgeable in all aspects of ocean racing. Ian is an experienced Atlantic rower. If there is a question or a problem, they have answered it or seen it before; Ian has probably either fixed it or rowed with it and they all know what to do to make preparation for the race as easy as possible. They are a great team to work with.

The safety of the rowers is absolutely the first and key consideration of the Atlantic Campaigns team. For this reason, the rules and stipulations are detailed and very extensive. Race officer Ian Couch is a respected scrutineer who is tough on competitors for their own good. Rigorous checks on people, boats and equipment are carried out six months before the race and then again, even more thoroughly, in La Gomera before a crew is allowed to cross the start line.

There are simply no exceptions permitted. The rules are the same for everyone but in order to identify any possible advantage we needed to examine and understand the rules completely. We would comply, but we wanted to find the most efficient way to comply.

The race rules run to over 100 pages of regulations and standards. Every aspect of the crew, boat, equipment and preparation is specified and must be met in full. The regulations include:

- ➡ RYA training in all aspects of maritime laws and practices.
- ➡ Qualification in: RYA Sea Survival, RYA First Aid at Sea, RYA Navigation and Seamanship.
- ➡ Ocean rowing certificate of competence.
- ➡ VHF radio usage licence.
- ➡ All electronic equipment navigation and safety equipment compliance and registration:
  - ⇨ GPS – Global Positioning System; supports location and navigation
  - ⇨ AIS – automatic identification system; transceiver which tracks and monitors vessel movements and advises of any likely collisions with other marine traffic
  - ⇨ EPIRB – emergency position-indicating radio beacon; an emergency locator beacon mounted on the boat, deployed in an emergency to signal the need for immediate rescue
  - ⇨ PLB – personal locator beacon; mounted on rower's safety harness to provide location signal in case of loss overboard.
- ➡ Boat build compliance and structural survey documentation.
- ➡ Practical demonstration of competence to use the boat and all equipment.
- ➡ Documents including medical and dental health statements, bereavement forms (who the race officer should contact if you die during the race, also whether you wish to be informed if a related party dies while you are at sea).

That does not include any of the additional checks on the hundreds of mandatory items, measurements and boat fitments which would be scrutineered in La Gomera before the race start. On top of that is the checking of the food and emergency water supply, which must meet a minimum specified standard for calorie count, quantity and content.

Failure to comply with even one item would result in the boat being prevented from starting the race. While it does seem frustrating to have to administer detail and documents while we were more focused on rowing preparation, it was a critically important checklist. Nobody wanted to find that we had forgotten a vital piece of survival equipment, or worse not know how to use it if we were in difficulty 1,000 miles from shore.

Our approach was to ensure that we achieved full compliance at the earliest possible stage. By making sure that we had passed our qualifications, organised our kit, ordered our food and knew how to use our equipment, we could really focus our time on the aspects which could give us an advantage and make the boat go faster.

We wanted to spend as much time as possible rowing together as a crew. This was where we would begin to find the opportunities to improve. Each time we rowed we learned something new. Getting out in the boat was the key.

4: NOTES FOR BUSINESS

Extraordinary performance begins with extraordinary engagement. Once the vision of success has been established and communicated, it should be clear what success will look like, what it will sound like and what it will feel like. Everyone in the team has a role to play to deliver that success. Now every individual has the opportunity to become excited and get engaged in the process.

Leaders should address any fear of change by discussing the new status the team are striving for, encouraging excitement about the freedom to make real and substantial change. The action plan must be shared and discussed, making it easy for the team to explore, examine and contribute to it. Invite comments and be totally inclusive of all ideas – let people dream, remove limitations. Encourage further contributions by widely communicating the successes of an individual's suggestions and improvements.

Leaders must create a positive culture and invite team members to move quickly towards the execution of the plan. Achieving a world-class level of performance is not easy and challenges will arise. Those very challenges are opportunities for growth. A rapid and productive approach to addressing challenges will move the organisation forward. Make heroes of the high-performing teams by praising their creativity and response to a challenge. Recognise that a positive approach can be transferable to other areas.

Prioritise, prioritise, prioritise
Do not aim to do everything at once. Through a workshop process, leaders should identify all activities which will need to be completed on the journey to world class. Agree a priority ranking with the team and discard the lower 50 per cent of the activities. Reprioritise the remaining 50 per cent and select half for urgent action. Concentrate on the delivery of the top 25 per cent.

Count every day

Do not build a plan which measures progress in months; rather, implement a detailed 100-day kick-off plan focused on the priority activities identified. Use this to raise energy levels and demonstrate activity. Support the 100-day plan with a 1,000-day plan designed to drive the development to world class. Projects should be scheduled in days and performance assessed every 10 days.[6]

Move quickly, make mistakes quickly, learn quickly

Rapid implementation of positive change will energise the organisation. Not every project will go smoothly but if it goes wrong use that experience as a learning opportunity. Back up, review, reconsider and then go forwards again. Share the learnings across the organisation.

Most limitations are self-imposed

Leading teams to high performance requires a recognition that fresh ideas and constructive challenges are a positive aspect of progress. Invite the team to consider how they would achieve results which are many times greater than that which is in the plan. Encourage debate which identifies creativity and challenges any limitations in the existing organisational mindset.

Be consistent

Leaders must always set a positive example, be approachable and consistent in their response to challenges. Confidence and positive belief are energy forms which transfer to others. Leaders should pass on praise easily, making heroes of those who have made a significant contribution.

---

6 See Gaskell, *Inspired Leadership*.

Get better and bigger will follow

Do not focus the plan on the delivery of a set of short-term trading figures or operational numbers. Focus efforts on delivering significant improvements to the entire organisation in a structured and prioritised manner. The objective is to build a world-class organisation. Achieve that and financial performance will improve in parallel.

5 BUILD YOUR SPACESHIP

At sea, I learned how little a person needs, not how much.

— Robin Lee Graham

Fewer people have rowed across an ocean than have flown in space. That's not to compare the two in terms of technology or complexity, but one direct similarity is that everything on board the vessel has to serve a purpose. In a racing situation, there is simply no allowance made for items which do not increase performance. With five big guys and our food and mandatory equipment alone, just finding stowage space on an eight-metre boat was going to be a real challenge. With a race to win we would be looking to reduce weight in every way possible.

Matt and I had learned from previous expeditions that nothing weighs nothing. If you add a couple of luxuries or items that 'may be useful', then you have another kilogram, and then another. Before you realise it, your carried weight has increased substantially. We intended to be ruthless in what was allowed onto the boat. The role of boat quartermaster was delegated to Matt, who was not going to allow a single item on board that he hadn't approved. This was an area where we believed we could take an advantage over many of the other boats which would be carrying luxuries, spares or even equipment that they would never need.

Our approach was to meticulously consider every aspect of the boat long before we got to the start of the race. Our objective was simple: conduct a detailed analysis of the combination of boat, equipment, food, kit and personnel and then determine how to reduce weight, improve efficiency and make the operation of the boat better and faster. We could not out-row, but we would out-plan.

Know what you want

The boat that we would choose for the race needed to meet the fundamental requirements of being strong, safe and thoroughly tested. It had to be efficient in operation and effective in transferring oar power into forward motion. It had to conform to all of the race regulations without question, as we had no time to waste debating rules with the race officer during scrutineering. It had to be capable of carrying five rowers and all essential kit and it had to be available at a sensible cost.

The cost of the boat was a consideration because we were self-funding our entry into the race. Any money we raised from the generosity of the sponsors who supported the Ocean5 project would be for the benefit of the charity we were supporting. The cost of entering the race, preparation, training, boat, travel, food and equipment would be met from our own pockets. There was a range of boats available at all price points. Some of the used boats were very inexpensive – but saving £10,000 probably wouldn't feel like such a wise choice if the boat sank 500 miles from shore. At the other end of the price scale, we were aware that some crews had retained a marine architect and a boatyard to build a boat to their own design. Any new design would have to be thoroughly tested for seaworthiness, safety (including their ability to self-right if capsized) and certified by specialist authorities. While a new design may be faster, it was not guaranteed. What a new design did guarantee was a substantial increase in budget and a longer timescale. We didn't have the scope for either.

We wanted a proven design which was also technologically state of the art and included the latest equipment and met all regulations. We appreciated that proven *and* including the latest technology was somewhat of a contradiction but we wanted a continuously improved successful design.

Find a partner who understands

After researching the performance of various boats in previous races we narrowed our focus of potential boat suppliers. Finally, we selected a manufacturer with enormous experience of building successful ocean rowing boats that we felt would provide excellent advice and work with us to make the modifications we wanted to improve boat operation and speed.

Rannoch Adventure is based in Burnham-on-Crouch, Essex. The business is led by Charlie Pitcher and Angus Collins, who are both pre-eminent sailors and ocean rowers. Charlie has been a member of the British America's Cup team and a member of the crew which won the Admiral's Cup. He has twice set the world record for the fastest solo row across the Atlantic. Angus has set world records for rowing across both the Atlantic and the Indian Oceans. It is fair to say that they really understand the needs of ocean rowers. They also build first-class ocean rowing boats.

Rannoch have been building and improving ocean rowing boats for a number of years. We shared our approach to the race with Charlie and Angus and explained that we intended to be as competitive as we absolutely could be and that we hoped to break the world record for a five-man crossing. They were nothing but hugely supportive as we explained that we would be looking for the latest technical innovation to support our record attempt. Charlie patiently showed us around a number of used boats and explained where technology had improved each model year. Some of the used boats had been modified by previous owners with differing degrees of success and benefit. It quickly became clear that if we were to acquire a boat which met our specification, and not spend time and money undoing a previous crew's modifications, we needed to buy a new boat. While this was an increase in the initial purchase price of about 20 per cent, it would require less modification work and would be worth more when we sold it on after the race.

Get the right kit for the job

We selected a new Rannoch R45. It is a tried and tested design with an excellent record for performance and safety and a heritage of continuous improvement. The R45 is a glass fibre-reinforced resin-hulled ocean rowing boat suitable for crews of three to five rowers. Designed to move efficiently through the water, it has minimal hydrodynamic drag and looks more like a glider aeroplane fuselage than a rowing boat. The boat has an overall length of 28 ft/8.6 m with a beam of 6 ft/1.8 m and a draft of 1 ft/0.3 m. Fully loaded with crew and equipment, the boat weighs 2,072 lb/940 kg.

The row deck has three rowing stations and a small cabin at each end. The cabins are designed to provide shelter and are approximately the size of a reasonable car boot. Two rowers can fit in each cabin – just – before the cabin space is compromised by the gear necessary for the crossing. Stowage is available in sealed lockers under the row deck and smaller lockers under the floor of the cabins. The boat is fitted with a desalination unit which converts seawater into drinking water, a suite of electronic navigation and communication equipment and navigation lights. All of this equipment runs on electricity from batteries which are recharged by solar panels mounted on the roof of the cabins.

Begin with the best – and improve it

Pete Goss[7] is a world-renowned sailor and a good friend of mine. He has raced in the Vendée Globe solo non-stop round the world yacht race, skippered a boat in the round-the-world British Steel Challenge and built and then sailed a Cornish lugger from Cornwall to Australia. In 1997 he was awarded the title World Sailor of the Year.[8] It is fair to say that he knows quite a bit about sailing! Some years ago, we walked to the North Pole together and one evening in our tent we were discussing his approach to preparing for a big sailing race. His advice was 'get the boat early, put her in the garden and live in her, get to know her, find the problems areas and deal with them, find the sharp corners and smooth them, learn how everything works and how to repair it, make sure everything is where you need it to be'. We took his advice.

Journal, April 27th 2019

Sam, Matt and I at the Rannoch open day to check out build progress on our boat and meet other crews. Looking to pick up tips and ideas. Rannoch team are extremely helpful and supportive. Hearing stories about when it all goes right and people break records, and when it all goes wrong and people break. Very clear that we have a lot to learn before we hit the Atlantic... there's just so much that we don't know.

---

7 See www.petegoss.com
8 See www.sailing.org/worldsailor/1997

We collected our new boat from Rannoch 400 days before the race was due to begin. We now had several months to follow Pete's approach and find opportunities to improve our performance.

Each time we trained with the boat we looked for areas where we could make adjustments which would improve our performance when in the race. Modifications were considered if they could improve operating efficiency, save time, or make the boat go faster. We also looked for ways to improve crew comfort – that being a very relative term in an open rowing boat at sea – but we needed to maximise our chances of sleep, nutrition and relaxation when not actually rowing.

The enhancements and improvements we made included:

➡ Lead acid batteries replaced by gel batteries – better performance, less susceptible to damage if not closely monitored. Improved safety and reduced effort.

➡ Drinking water system rerouted to allow reservoir filling inside or outside the cabin. Allowed the crew to sleep as the reservoir fills. Improved safety and reduced time and effort.

➡ Storage shelf system built above rudder housing – increased storage, fast access to first-line tools and equipment. Reduced time and effort for repairs.

➡ Solar panel roof rack designed and installed – easy protection for auxiliary solar panel. Reduced time and effort.

➡ Storage nets fitted all around – easy access to frequent-use equipment. Reduced time.

➡ Fast-release lanyards for drinking bottles installed – easy to refill, not lost over the side.

➡ Jackstays tightened (safety lines) – improved safety and increased speed of moving around boat.

➡ Non-slip tape applied to row deck – improved safety and increased speed of moving around the boat.

- ➡ Auxiliary radar reflector installed – improved our visibility to big boats. Increased safety and reduced monitoring time.
- ➡ Sized spanners fitted to each piece of kit – rapid access and repair in case of failure.
- ➡ Lanyard on each piece of row deck kit – reduced chances of loss. Reduced time and effort.
- ➡ Platform for Jetboil water heater installed – increased safety. Reduced time and effort.
- ➡ Steel vacuum flasks positioned in each cabin – increased safety and efficiency of preparing meals.
- ➡ Rowing foot straps replaced – reduced chances of blisters (not completely effective!).
- ➡ Seat cushions – various! There's a whole story in the selection of padding for the seats but we still ended up in acute pain because of infected bum cheek blisters!

In addition to these modifications, each piece of equipment on the boat was considered for utility and value. While we made many adjustments, we did not automatically move to the latest technology. The desalination unit was mission critical and despite the manufacturer Schenker launching a new generation of products in advance of the race, we decided to remain with a previous generation product as it was tried and tested over a number of years. Failure of the water maker would have been the end of our race. The new generation was 5 kg lighter but unproven in race conditions. We considered it high risk and decided to save 5 kg somewhere else.

Learn how to use it

Carrying equipment that you cannot use effectively is a double waste – it is increased weight as well as the increased distraction of sorting out a query at sea. We were highly selective in the equipment that we carried. Critical equipment that must work at all times and that each member of the crew must be able to use, even in difficult conditions, include the AIS system, the VHF radio and the navigation system. The satellite phone acted as a backup from which we could make calls to any telephone number, including emergency contacts.

The most important of our systems on a day-to-day, and especially night-to-night, basis was the AIS. Our boat was an eight-metre-long plastic object with the top of the cabin standing one metre above the waterline. Even when the water is calm, the swells are over a metre high and our radar signature was minimal. We are therefore potentially invisible to the navigator of a cruise liner or merchant vessel. The bridge of a 400-metre-long container ship may be 50 metres above the waterline. They would be moving at 24 knots and covering three miles in about seven minutes. If they were bearing down on us that would not give us long to react, especially at night with two crew rowing and three sleeping.

We are moving at two knots and affected by the prevailing wind and current; we cannot easily change direction. Even if we tried, the ship could easily change its direction of travel and still run over us without noticing. AIS sends out a signal telling all local ships who we are (tiny plastic rowing boat) and where we are (that dot three miles ahead at bearing 350 degrees) and our direction of travel (we may be rowing directly across the ship's path). The AIS is designed to alert the ship's navigator before they have a visual sighting. The system allows us to set up an 'intruder alarm' to warn if any other vessel is going to get within a set distance of our boat. With a ten-mile setting, any incursion closer than that would be signalled with a loud alarm, at which point we would use the VHF radio to speak to the vessel and confirm that they had seen us.

During the race we had radio contact with five commercial

vessels. Each one had already spotted us via AIS and one evening a cruise liner decelerated from 25 to 10 knots as it passed close by, for which we were very grateful. We could imagine the captain of the cruise liner saying to his guests over dinner, 'Ladies and gentlemen, we are 1,200 miles from land and hope you are enjoying your dinner and fine wine. If you look to starboard you will see some lunatics starving themselves in a rowing boat...'

Our effective use of the navigation system was critical if we were to take advantage of the benefits available from the prevailing weather, winds and currents. Each day we would use the satellite phone to speak to our shore-based weather router who would interpret weather reports and forecasts and advise target coordinates for us to row to. Using the navigation equipment intelligently allowed us to be aggressive with our routing and competitive with our rowing. As part of our approach to the race, we agreed that we would choose to take a more direct route even if it meant facing bad weather and rough seas.

During the race we didn't see another rowing boat from one hour after the start for the rest of the race. From our daily routing calls, we knew where they were, their bearing (direction of travel) and speed and what the ambient weather was for each of them. We used that information but did not waste time on their progress. We concentrated on making our boat go faster and more directly towards the finish line. The old expedition adage is 'look after your kit, and your kit will look after you'. A key part of increasing our competitiveness was to have the correct equipment, know how to use it and then let it do its work. All our efforts were focused on pulling the oars. We reminded ourselves that we were not going to out-row, but we could out-plan and out-navigate.

5: NOTES FOR BUSINESS

Building a world-class organisation can be the result of a new start-up, the turnaround of a business in difficulty or the challenge of reinvigorating an existing organisation. Whichever it is, once the vision of success is clear, the first responsibility of the leadership team is to engage the team in the development of a clear 100-day mobilisation plan, followed by a 1,000-day development plan which is designed to create a world-class organisation founded on solid principles.

Every action within the plan must be essential to achieve a defined goal. There is no time or resource available to pursue goals which are not totally aligned to delivering the agreed goal. World-class performance is achieved by the relentless pursuit of specific goals for each aspect of the organisation. Those goals must be defined, refined and agreed. Any activity outside that which is absolutely necessary to deliver these goals should be considered a distraction. The best organisations are ruthless when identifying activities which will not support the delivery of the plan. The isolation and removal of actions, projects or tasks which do not contribute to the speedy delivery of the goal is one of the most effective leadership techniques.

To be most efficient when building a successful future, appreciate that the world is already populated with examples of excellence. Seek them out and apply them to your own purposes. Do not reinvent the wheel (or build your own accounting or CRM system – I have seen companies waste time and resources doing both). Recognise that real value is created at the point where the client touches the company and that it is the experience of what the process delivers that is important and not the process itself.

Study the market. Who are your clients?
Be brutally honest in mapping your products or services to the needs of your potential audience. Contact them, speak to them, explore their needs and interrogate your organisation's ability to deliver to their requirements.

Identify world-class businesses
Look for organisations which are very similar or very different to your own. Examine the operation of key competitors and identify their strengths (ignore their weaknesses), learn from organisations very different to your own. What processes, systems, people or products that you identify could you use in your own organisation?

There is only one version of the truth
Be efficient. Make sure that your analysis is impartial, detailed and accurate. Do not waste your time with filtered information or biased feedback. Building a world-class organisation requires focus on real facts with decisions made accordingly.

Consider the options: reorganise, re-energise, rebuild
When aligning the current organisation to the future vision of world class, examine business units and processes separately. Consider whether the required improvement can be achieved by the reorganisation of the current process, the re-energising (inspiring, coaching or changing) of the leadership team, or whether a full rebuild of the unit is necessary.

Prepare to make substantial changes
Change the thinking, change the limits. Develop a culture which accepts effective change as a positive process – but do not make changes which are not necessary. Reorganise and re-energise are usually quicker than rebuild. Always focus on the most efficient route to long-term success.

Focus on getting the basics right, first time every time

Set your fundamental performance goals (logistics, delivery, service response, etc.) at a level which most organisations do not dare to pursue. Invite the leadership and the organisation to innovate to achieve those goals. Companies which can consistently deliver the basics at the highest level will win customer loyalty and space to progress towards market leadership.

6 CHECK, CHECK AND CHECK AGAIN

It's the little details that are vital. Little things make big things happen.

– John Wooden

After more than two years of preparation, we arrived in La Gomera. It was 12 days before the race was due to start and this was our opportunity for final preparations. We had booked self-catering accommodation away from the marina and away from our families. This was the first time that the crew had lived together for longer than the time we had spent at sea on two- or three-day training sessions. It was a period of calm before the storm and our opportunity to prepare mentally, to stay prepared physically and to ensure everything worked logistically. Our apartment was high on a hill with an awe-inspiring view of the ocean and the horizon. It was difficult to grasp that in a few days we would be rowing over that horizon into the unknown.

We needed to focus and prepare. Loading, scrutineering and checking the boat would take time but we felt we were in good shape and would have time each day to relax. Chris,

Sam and Will found a gym and distracted themselves there, Matt concentrated on gentle jogging and lots of sleep. I was completely immersed in a business crisis. With dreadful timing the UK government had called a snap election for the day that the race would start. I had been driving the turnaround of a technology company for the previous two years and as we had made progress, we had reached agreement with a major investor that they would inject critical funding into the company. Unfortunately, the investor had suddenly announced that the funding would now depend on the outcome of the election. This meant that I was totally distracted for some hours each day keeping the business open and my fingers crossed.

Look like you mean it

Our boat had been shipped ahead of us. A line of 36 ocean rowing boats perfectly lined up in the Atlantic Campaigns boat park was an impressive sight. Suddenly it struck us that this was all real and we were going to start to row across the Atlantic in only a few days. The boat park was filled with all the other competitors, their boats and their equipment. The air crackled with energy and excitement.

The race officers' welcome meeting confirmed the schedule for the ten days before the race and reminded all crews that any boat failing scrutineering would not be allowed to start. There was a lot to do but it was clear that some crews were far more prepared than others.

There was an atmosphere of friendly banter and camaraderie, but also a gentle rivalry between the teams. Without being too obvious we walked around the boat park searching for tips or clever ideas that we could adapt to our own boat and preparation. We were looking for any and every single opportunity to find each one per cent gain, those small

It all starts with a plan

Getting the crew and boat together for the first time

First training sessions dodging the big ships in the Solent

Lots of training meant lots of
overnight rowing

First training session showed how far
I had to go to be race ready

Almost 500 kg of food ready to be packed into the boat

Lady Jayne ready to be packed into a container and shipped to La Gomera

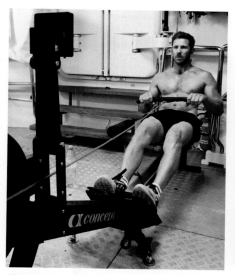

Training wherever possible. Chris in the engine room of a superyacht

The crew lifted over two million kgs during training

VHF radio is key to communication with approaching ships

Immersion suits would help us survive should we abandon ship

Leaving the UK, looking like a team

San Sebastián de La Gomera packed with ocean rowing boats

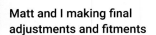

Chris and Sam antifoul the hull to reduce drag

Matt and I making final adjustments and fitments

Short row out from the harbour before the race

Final briefing to the crews, one hour before the race start

The Ocean5 official team photograph

Five minutes to go – the strongest bonds are forged under the greatest pressure

Crossing the start line with a reminder of how far to the finish

Morning after the storm, para anchor still trailing as we deal with the damage

Matt and Sam make up for miles lost during the storm

Matt and I keeping up the pace as the weather improves

Sam and Matt negotiating huge following swells

Will and Sam enjoy sunrise after a tough small hours shift

Sam and I enjoying a push from the following seas

Chris and
Will fighting a
typical squall

Sam and Matt
into the sunset
for another
overnight shift

Chris and Will enjoy a wonderful sunrise

improvements that we might be able to use to give us the edge.

Back at our own boat we had a small ceremony to perform. Up until this point our whole project had been known as The Ocean5 and we hadn't actually given a name to our boat. We had discussed all sorts of alternatives but one day we realised that we each had a lady named Jayne somewhere in our family. In my case it was my sister Jayne, who sadly lost a long battle against leukaemia some years ago.

Matt and I had walked to the geographic North and South Poles in her memory and the generosity of our sponsors had allowed us to fund the construction of a treatment ward at the North Wales Cancer Centre. This was a different challenge but since there is a strong tradition of naming boats after special women it was agreed that we should name ours Lady Jayne. We held a brief naming ceremony, applied the Lady Jayne nameplate and knew that our respective Jaynes would be in our thoughts as we rowed.

We were still speaking to sponsors and potential sponsors, using social media and photographs of the amazing sights around us to further raise our profile and sponsors' interest and raise as much funding as possible for our charity. As planned, we presented ourselves every day in our branded team kit. We aimed to look like a team, sound like a team and behave like a team.

Our presentation as a team was partly intended to demonstrate confidence and self-belief. We wanted to look like winners.

Journal, November 30th 2019

La Gomera looks similar to our recce last year but excitement levels feel higher. First time here for Matt and Will. Lady Jayne looks really good lined up with 35 other boats. Our apartment is great with an amazing view out to sea. Friends and family arriving in a few days so chance to finalise prep and also have a few days' rest. I'm completely preoccupied raising funding for one of my companies. The coincidence of the race and the funding round could not be more inconvenient... very stressful.

We had arrived in La Gomera feeling that we were well prepared. But the race officers had made it very clear to everyone that you could never be fully prepared for what we were about to experience and that the real competition was 3,000 miles of unpredictable Atlantic Ocean. We knew that the ocean would not care how we looked, only how we performed. If we meant to win this race it was all very well looking like a team but it was more important that we performed like a team.

Make sure you qualify

We spent three days carefully packing the boat and waxing and applying antifoul to the underside of the hull. The coating is critical to keep the nasties away – slime, weed, barnacles and other creatures enjoy growing under a boat and either slow it down or eat it away, or both. We lovingly applied three coats to the entire hull in the anticipation that a super slippery finish would help to increase our average speed. Another one per cent gain.

Working out where every piece of kit, food and equipment would fit was a three-dimensional jigsaw. Each locker, storage space, nook and cranny were filled with food or essential equipment. We kept a packing map as it was critical to know exactly where everything was. The next time we may need it, it could be the middle of the night, completely dark and in a heavy sea. The heaviest equipment that we packed was the food. The food we used was freeze-dried expedition ration packs. They are pretty bombproof and will last for years but to be edible they must be mixed with (ideally, hot) water and eaten after about ten minutes of rehydration. The drinking water is produced by the desalination unit built into the boat and powered by electricity generated by solar panels on the roof of the cabins. Our rerouting of the water pipes meant that we could collect water into a jerry can in the cabin while we slept rather than have one person control a 25-litre container as it filled on a rolling deck. Another one per cent gain.

Each main meal averaged 550 calories. Each person was allocated four meals per day, plus a snack pack of nuts, chocolate, cake, dried fruit, protein bars, pork scratchings, jelly babies or anything else the rower fancied (the higher the calorie count the better). That equated to a total of 5,200 calories per person per day. For a crew of five rowers, the total calories onboard were circa 5,200 x 5 = 26,000 x 60 days which is 1.6 million calories. Each rower would be burning 7,000 calories per day or 2.1 million calories for all of us for the 60 days. In addition, in case we had to abandon ship into the life raft, we carried 10 days' worth of emergency wet rations of cold pasta or chicken curry which would be eaten straight out of a squeezy bag, plus 50 litres of emergency drinking water. On risk of disqualification, the wet rations could not be touched except in a life-or-death situation. The total weight of the food on the boat was more than 400 kilograms.

The boat was scrutineered, the kit was scrutineered, the food was scrutineered, the crew's knowledge of the equipment was scrutineered. Every item on board had been checked and counted twice, and then twice more. Finally, scrutineering was finished with a pass and our race number was awarded. Now we were confirmed as competitors. We had qualified and we were ready for the race.

Prepare, prepare, prepare

Setting to sea and then realising that we had forgotten to bring something important would be extremely frustrating and could damage our record attempt. It was critical that we didn't let the excitement distract us from checking every detail of every piece of equipment – again. During the preparation phase we had a checklist of 437 items which were ticked off as each item was checked and loaded on board Lady Jayne.

A lot of thought had gone into the stowing and positioning of food and equipment. As we ate our way through the food the balance of the boat would alter as weight was removed. We would move food and equipment around during the voyage to maintain the efficient trim and rowing of the boat. Another one per cent gain.

Journal, December 11th 2019

Last night before the start. Watching a beautiful sunset from our crew apartment. Strange to think we will row into that sunset tomorrow. Crew chat about compromise of race performance against watching wildlife. Everyone torn — we want to watch whales but also win the race. Confirmed the world record comes first but we will pause briefly if we have close encounters with big fish (mammals!). Mood is good but sleep is going to be difficult... we have no real idea what we will face over that horizon.

We had prepared and mounted laminated process charts and allowed for quick changes to rowing shift patterns in case one or more of the crew were incapacitated. We had laminated charts for radio use, emergency calls and sponsor contact information. We had been warned that we would go a bit mad at sea as a result of the lack of sleep and continuous physical exertion. The process charts were to help us to make decisions, or place emergency calls, if we were in a stressful or emergency situation completely exhausted and not able to think straight.

After careful consideration we had chosen, in some situations, to duplicate essential kit prioritising operating efficiency over weight. Moving about the boat at any time was extremely difficult due to the lack of space. Should there be a storm during darkness it was not only extremely difficult but also exceptionally dangerous to try to move back and forth along the row deck stepping over rowers and oars. Visibility would be near zero and with huge waves continuously surging across the deck it would be very easy for one of us to lose our footing and be washed overboard. We tied duplicate spanners and hand tools to the pieces of kit that they fitted. This, together with some fixed torches, meant that we would not have to move to the cabin to find the appropriate tools and could quickly repair equipment at night in a stormy ocean. For speed of racing, any maintenance had to happen quickly and easily – and safely. Another one per cent gain.

While we wanted to be as competitive as possible, safety was our overriding concern in all decisions. Throwing ropes were positioned at diagonally opposite points on the boat. We would always be wearing a safety harness which was tethered to safety lines on the boat but if one of us did get knocked overboard we needed to recover them quickly. We didn't want to waste time manoeuvring the boat, so a quickly thrown and caught rope would reduce the time lost. Of course, there was always the risk that the crew member could not be recovered, or that they were recovered drowned. After discussing all 'what if' scenarios we agreed that in such a case the race authorities would be advised, the body (if recovered) would be stowed and the rest of the crew would aim to carry on rowing to Antigua and win the race. Our determination was absolute and sharing that brought us closer as a team.

We were set to go.

On the last day of preparation, Charlie Pitcher, MD of Rannoch and holder of numerous ocean rowing records, remarked that The Ocean5 were looking really good as a team and he thought that Lady Jayne was the best-prepared boat in the fleet.

We were flattered that Charlie would make such a comment. Now we would have to do Lady Jayne justice and row her to the front of the fleet across the Atlantic!

6: NOTES FOR BUSINESS

Building a world-class organisation should feel exciting. The role of the leader is to share the excitement and invite the team to share a journey towards an extraordinary future. A key aspect of leadership is the ability to confidently share a vision for the organisation which is compelling and inspires the team members to want to build something that they can look back on with pride.

A compelling vision coupled with the way that the leadership team acts will determine the culture of the organisation. Culture can be defined as how the organisation actually works; what the team does, what they say, how they behave. Crucially, the culture of the organisation defines the way that team members act when they have the freedom to work in an unsupervised situation. That shared culture becomes the everyday reality of the way that team members communicate internally, how they deliver products and services and how they respond to customers.

A world-class experience is enjoyed by the client when the anticipated attention to product or service detail is delivered. Creating this level of service begins with a leader who is seen to be passionate about delivering the details. Such leadership builds a culture where focus on the detail is shared and important tasks can be delegated to the people who know how best to deliver them. Shared ownership builds trust, increases confidence and stimulates innovation.

Understand what your customers care about
Gather clear and accurate information about what your customers expect and what they value. Make sure that you carefully consider, study and deliver each minor detail that creates a greater experience and memorable relationship for the customer with your product or service.

Wherever the client touches the organisation...

... must be world class: online, offline, product delivery, service support. The customer's impression of your business is an integrated result of a combination of experiences. Attention to detail creates a standard and consistent experience and encourages brand loyalty.

Get it right first time, every time

Customers will remember most times when you have delivered a world-class service. But human nature is such that they will remember every time that you get it wrong. Ensure that the delivery of a world-class experience is process driven and plan your business accordingly. Deliver the basics especially well.

Never stop learning

Creating the best company involves continuous improvement in all areas of the organisation. Observing and learning from other organisations is key to driving innovation. Appointing new team members will bring fresh ideas and experience but be aware that existing employees with deep experience will also show creativity and a fresh approach if the culture is supportive and encouraging.

World class in three dimensions

World class is experienced in three dimensions. Consider what the customer will see in your organisation, what they will hear, what they will feel. All of these sensory facets must be aligned if they are to provide a superior experience. Take time to consider how each facet is developed and demonstrated in your organisation.

Price is not a number...

... it is an experience. Clients will be attracted and retained by a business which provides a complete brand experience. A world-class experience will be valued at a far higher level than an average experience. Define the key elements of your brand experience to be notable and exceptional. Do not be afraid to innovate – but do not conduct tests of ideas on your audience. Innovations must be proven to add value.

7 INTO THE GREAT UNKNOWN

It is impossible to win the race unless you venture to run, impossible to win the victory unless you dare to battle.

– Richard M DeVos

Following rumours of storms and a delayed start, Thursday 12 December dawned as a beautiful day. The previous evening, we had eaten dinner together with all of our families and then the five of us returned to our crew apartment. We had discussed until late what our ultimate goal should be – was it the world record or was it a world-class experience? Would we pause to watch the sea life if a whale or similar came close to the boat, or would we just keep chasing the record? Recognising that this row could be a once-in-a-lifetime experience, we agreed to pause and photograph the wildlife – and then row faster to make up lost time! We were set.

Our last onshore breakfast was porridge and high-calorie snacks as we didn't know when we would next get the chance to eat. The mood in the crew house was excited but nervous. After almost 1,000 days of preparation and training we were confident in ourselves and in Lady Jayne. But even Chris, Sam and Will, the experienced mariners in our crew, who were used to being at sea in a 50-metre superyacht, were going into the unknown in an eight-metre open rowing boat.

We dressed in our team kit. Feeling good and intending to appear confident and look like a winning team. It was time to go.

Final call

The final pre-race safety and weather briefing brought all of the crews together for the last time. More than 50 rowers were crammed into the briefing marquee. All had spent years imagining and preparing for this moment. Each rower was following their dream and about to embark on the journey and undertaking of a lifetime. The atmosphere was a mix of anticipation, excitement and trepidation. The nervous energy in the room was palpable. The news from the weather monitoring team was good – the anticipated storm which had threatened to delay the start of the race had moved away and was expected to pass to the north of the fleet during the night or following day. Even better, a fresh north-easterly wind would help the boats to get out of the harbour and set south away from the rocks of La Gomera. Race officer Ian Couch reiterated the safety instruction one final time that rowers must be tethered to the boat at all times and with that command wished us luck. That was it... time to race.

The starting order was announced. The boats would go off one at a time and we had an hour before it was our turn to cross the start line and begin one of the biggest adventures of our lives. Everyone was in good spirits, with hundreds of families, friends, well-wishers and bemused tourists watching as the crews said their goodbyes. We climbed aboard Lady Jayne and calmly completed our final checks. Everything that could have been prepared was prepared. Now we had to believe in ourselves, our training and our planning. If it wasn't on board now or if we weren't prepared for it, whatever it was, it was too late.

The crowds cheered as each boat crossed the start line, sent on their way with a chorus of air horns and fireworks. With ten minutes to go, skipper Chris called a crew huddle. We shook hands, wished each other well and recommitted to our agreed principles:

➡ Start as friends, finish as friends.
➡ Be kind.

We knew that at some point in the crossing we were each going to have a bad day, or make a mistake, or feel ill, afraid or worse. At those times we would need to support our crewmates because the next day it could be our turn to have the bad day. We had heard of crews becoming completely dysfunctional due to internal arguments. We had discussed those situations and were determined that we would not let that happen to us.

As we settled into our rowing seats, we heard the good wishes and kind words shouted to us from families and friends and also from people in the crowd who we had never met, but who felt that just by watching us row away they were part of something quite special. It was a human celebration of passion, determination – and a little bit of madness. We had previously agreed our starting roles; Chris would hand steer us out of the harbour, avoiding the passenger ferries coming into and out of the port and keeping us off the rocks. Sam, Will and I were rowing. Matt was monitoring the boat, systems and radio.

With a two-minute warning, the race director pushed Lady Jayne off the pontoon and we began rowing towards the start. It was time to focus. With AC/DC playing 'Thunderstruck' at full volume through our onboard speaker (one concession to weight – minus one per cent; inspirational and energising – plus two per cent!) we crossed the start line. As we left the marina, we felt the breeze coming off the mountains and the energy of the waves underneath Lady Jayne. Now it was serious. We had become part of the world of the ocean and the horizon suddenly looked a long way away. We focused on rowing steadily and efficiently. Check, check and check again. Chris completed another round of checking the radio, AIS, navigation and autohelm settings as we watched the crowds and marina fade behind us into the distance. Thirty-six boats had started the race but with our eyeline only one metre above the waterline and the ocean dancing to a gentle swell, we soon lost sight of our competitors. We would not see them again until after we had arrived in Antigua.

Go your own way

The morning briefing had recommended to all crews that they head south-west on leaving the marina. That way the anticipated stormy weather was expected to pass well north of the fleet. The majority of the boats followed that advice, aiming south-west to eventually pick up the trade winds. The Ocean5, however, had a secret weapon and he was called Stokey Woodall. Stokey is a highly respected ocean sailor, author (and raconteur – if you have an hour or three!) who has sailed over 350,000 miles across the earth's oceans. He is the principal of International Ocean Services (IOS), which provides weather routing services to some of the world's most important sea traffic.

We knew that to be in with a chance of setting a record, helpful weather would be critical. We would have to find and utilise every single kilogram of propulsion that we could get from the prevailing wind and sea state. Our intention was that Stokey would provide the information which would allow us to make the best decisions possible for our route across the Atlantic. Daily calls to Stokey should provide a very detailed weather map of current and forecast conditions for each rowing day. This would allow us to navigate to the route which would minimise distance (another one per cent gain) and maximise the availability of following winds (another one or even two per cent gain).

Journal, December 12th 2019

2 hours out from La Gomera and settling down. Started well but headed away from the fleet. Haven't seen another boat for about an hour. Saying goodbye to families and friends was tough but we had so much to do that there was no time to think about it. Laughing as we crossed the start line with AC/DC blasting through our speaker and fireworks going off above us. Just off the oars and now looking back towards the start, which is fading into the horizon. Slight feeling of apprehension about what's ahead of us. Team in good spirits... water a bit choppy but ok.

Stokey's advice on day one was contrary to that provided by the race organisers. He felt that The Ocean5 should head west rather than follow the fleet south-west. His logic was that we should be able to use the power of the gathering storm to the north to enjoy a push from the strong following winds. Recognising his knowledge and advice, we navigated west and settled into our regular rowing rota, two hours on, two hours off. Having spent many days training and living on Lady Jayne in British coastal waters, everything felt familiar yet still a little different. As the evening settled in, we passed the mandatory race waymark keeping us well away from the island of El Hierro and its dangerous rocks as our last sight of land disappeared from view. Previous rowers had warned us that by day three we would be so seasick and disorientated that we would just want to get off the boat, but that by day ten we would be loving it. That warning was far from our thoughts as we watched the sun sink beneath the horizon and headed into the dark unknown. The weather was blustery and generally giving us a push; so far, so good. We were comfortable and making strong progress. Morale was high, we were finding our rhythm and we were enjoying it.

7: NOTES FOR BUSINESS

Rebuilding an organisation or launching a new product, service or even complete company is an enormous undertaking. It is a huge challenge which requires careful planning, a clarity of purpose, determination, a huge amount of effort and a lot of courage. There are very many reasons never to begin to build something new. That's the key reason why most people don't try.

Thankfully there are many people who do. People who are brave enough to follow their ambition despite statistics quantifying that more than 90 per cent of new ventures will end in failure. There are new entrants to the markets every day; some are genuinely new ideas, others are a fresh take on a product or service already offered by many other companies. These new entrants or revitalised organisations are necessary to maintain commercial progress by challenging the established order and imposing change and innovation on the market.

One of the key attributes of those who successfully revitalise a moribund company or build a new enterprise is that they maintain a healthy disregard for the impossible. They must be prepared to accept setbacks while continuing to strive to deliver progress. They will constantly need to produce new ideas, fresh approaches and a determination to experiment and evolve their business with no fear of failure. Successful leaders enthusiastically accept that getting it wrong is part of eventually getting it right.

Imagine what could be possible
Every inspirational leader tends to be a dreamer first. Dreamers never start with the numbers; they start by imagining what the organisation could be and what it could deliver if there were no boundaries. Dare to be passionate, dare to break the rules, dare to focus on becoming world class while your competitors are concentrating on the mundane.

Decide what you are prepared to sacrifice

Building a world-class organisation is more than a full-time role. Only those leaders prepared to dedicate their full time and attention to the project will be successful. Be realistic about the expectations and demands that this project will place upon you and the team. Make clear decisions about what you are prepared to forego in your professional and personal life to deliver success in this project.

Develop a clear plan for success

Clearly define the goals and major aspects of the build process. Share the outline implementation plan with the team and actively engage them in the development of the details for specific areas. Share the responsibility by delegating clearly and comprehensively with simple and plain reporting mechanisms.

Be bold, make clear decisions

Gain momentum by making bold changes. Identify key areas with the greatest prospect for improvement and set expectations which require the focus of energy and resources. Encourage the team to overcome concerns by clear communication of the benefits which will result from achieving the change.

Never lose sight of the goal

Move quickly, learn quickly, make mistakes quickly and correct them. Do not be afraid to try new approaches. Recognise that every hour of running the operation and every revised process is a learning experience.

Create leaders at every level

Leaders build confidence and trust by being open, consistent and transparent. Leaders share responsibility and recognise that feedback is a crucial learning opportunity. Tasks should be delegated with agreed authority and accountability. Celebrate progress and learn from setbacks; the objective is to catch people in when projects go well, not catch people out when there are inevitable difficulties.

8 AND THEN IT ALL WENT WRONG!

Success is not final; failure is not fatal. It is the courage to continue that counts. If you're going through hell, keep going.

– Winston Churchill

The working area on the boat comprised the row deck. Measuring approximately four metres long by 1.5 metres wide, it was entirely covered by three rowing stations. Together with the tiny cabin at each end, this provided the total space within which we could row, shelter, sleep, wash, cook, eat and toilet. When we first started training in the boat this seemed to be an impossibly small area for five big guys to live in, but now it was our entire universe. As we settled into the routine a mindset shift had quickly taken place. Somehow the accommodation seemed to expand as we became familiar with every cubic centimetre of space available for storage and comfort. Privacy no longer existed; we were never more than half a metre away from the next person and very soon everyone had used the toilet bucket in full view of everyone else. Soon the close quarters and lack of space didn't seem an issue.

As our first night settled around us, we were making good

progress and enjoying the positive push of the anticyclonic winds from the weather system passing to our north. The sea was lumpy and the waves were becoming more random, but so far everything appeared to be going pretty well. Following Stokey's weather routing advice we were well to the north of the fleet and on track to cover 80 nautical miles in our first full day of rowing. This was an excellent result and suggested that we were holding our own in the fleet.

Don't ever get too comfortable

As the day ended and the darkness slowly deepened around us, we settled into Lady Jayne and our own little world. Since the light spill from the navigation lights on the boat dramatically reduced our night vision, we had learned during training that it was better to row with the lights turned off. That was probably against marine law and could perhaps be considered as unsafe but we always kept a sharp lookout for other ships. We also had the AIS system which, if it identified another vessel within ten miles, would raise a loud alarm, in which case we would quickly switch the navigation lights on. The ability to see the water and the approaching waves was key for us to row efficiently and safely.

Of course, to see clearly, we needed some light and at night that was provided either by the moon or the stars. As luck would have it, our first night of the crossing was going to be cloudy. As our visibility gradually reduced, it was clear that the weather was getting progressively worse. Soon it was impossible to tell how much worse it was likely to get, or to get a general idea of the sea state, as we were struggling to see anything beyond the huge swells and foam-topped waves which were surging past Lady Jayne.

Depending on the sea state and wind conditions, an ocean rowing boat with two rowers and friendly winds will average a speed of something approaching three knots (nautical miles per hour). The problem is that a weather system will travel at 20 knots or more. This simple fact meant that we could not outrun any difficult weather and would always be at the mercy of the prevailing conditions. We could see from the change in the cloud cover and the increasingly rough and surging sea state that the storm, previously forecast to pass us to the north, had turned south and was now overtaking and engulfing us. As the wind picked up, the sea became progressively more hostile and the wave direction more unpredictable. For much of the day we had been comfortable in our rowing and confident in our management of the boat. During the past hour that situation had totally changed.

Within what appeared to be only a few minutes, rowing became extremely difficult and even staying upright in the rowing seat was a battle as the wind and waves were striking the boat on the beam (side) before washing over the boat side and across the deck. We changed our heading to try to cope better with the waves but our forward speed fell and it felt as if the whole boat was being sucked into the boiling grey water. The size of the waves continued to grow until three- or four-metre-high surges of dark water were crashing into the boat, appearing without warning from every direction. Our visibility in the dark was almost zero and was made worse by the wind whipping up spray and the waves striking us as they flew across the deck. It was clear that we were now in the middle of the storm and that it was passing directly over us. Our situation had changed within 30 minutes from good progress and comfortable rowing to no progress and taking a pounding. Like most people I had never seen an Atlantic storm from the outside but now I was seeing one from the inside and the power of the water around us was awe inspiring.

Will and I dug in hard and rowed with all of our strength to keep control of the boat, make some forward motion and keep the autohelm engaged. To maintain a heading, the required compass bearing is entered into the electronic navigation system which drives an autohelm fixed to the tiller arm; this in turn moves the rudder. The autohelm needs the boat to maintain some forward motion or else it will disengage. If the autohelm were to disengage we would lose the ability to control the boat and Lady Jayne could be spun around in any direction by the force of the water and wind striking her. With waves containing thousands of tonnes of water continuously passing under, around and over the boat, the rowing had become a battle and it was gruelling work.

At the end of our two-hour shift, Will and I were exhausted and more than ready to swap with Chris and Matt. It was completely dark and the boat was pitching violently with heavy waves crashing across the deck. It was clear that this changeover was going to be difficult and would need careful coordination. To prevent water from entering the cabin and potentially capsizing the boat, we could only open the doors for the briefest of time. The rower on deck would watch the sea and try to judge the waves so that he could shout to the rower in the cabin when they felt there would be a brief gap before the next big wave arrived. The new rower would then quickly open the door, immediately tether their harness to the safety line, then climb out of the cabin locking the door behind them. Fixing onto the safety line was always our first action because not doing so and then losing a rower overboard into the storm-lashed sea would have been a fatal mistake. The tired rowers would then secure the oars and stand up to vacate the seat while passing the incoming rower on a lurching row deck. Seats, drinks bottles and snacks would all need to be swapped. The only handhold on deck was the nylon jackstay which ran the length of the boat but, being a four-metre-long length of nylon strapping, it swung back and forth as a rower held onto it.

We were performing the changeover while balancing on a tiny floating platform which was pitching in every direction, surrounded by a boiling ocean with huge waves and foaming water coming out of the impenetrable dark and striking the boat from every angle. As well as protecting themselves, the new rowers would need to quickly get control of the oars, which were in danger of being caught and whipped around by the waves. A four-metre-long carbon fibre oar, pivoting midway along its length and then caught by a wave, would quickly become a very dangerous weapon which could badly injure a rower, or worse, knock one of us overboard. While this was going on, the roaring noise of the crashing ocean was immense and with the wind whipping away our voices, communication became extremely difficult.

Coordinating our movement by hand signals, we manoeuvred around Chris and Matt as they got into the rowing seats. Will and I then moved carefully to opposite ends of the boat as we headed for the relative relief of our cabins. Again, we needed to time the opening of the cabin door to be between waves and then quickly swing ourselves through the small door before immediately locking it closed behind us. Opening the cabin door is one of the most dangerous moments on board an ocean rowing boat. If a wave swamps the boat while a cabin door is open, the cabin could flood. That would mean about two tonnes of water rushing in, damaging our equipment and possibly causing the boat to capsize. Crucially, if the cabin was filled with seawater, the boat would not be able to right itself and would stay capsized. Five guys swimming and clinging to an upturned hull in an Atlantic storm 30 miles from the nearest land, with no communication or possibility of rescue, would not be the ideal way to spend our first night at sea.

Take a rest when you can

Once off shift, regardless of what was going on outside the cabin, we needed to get some rest. The cabins are the size of a car boot and are crammed with equipment. There is just enough space for one person to lie down. The process now was: remove safety harness, take off wet clothes, mix up a hot meal from the Thermos of hot water and a ration pack, let meal soak, massage sore bits on the body, do some work on blisters, prepare clothes and gear to get dressed quickly for the next row shift, eat rehydrated food, check navigation coordinates and AIS, check satellite phone for messages, set up a bedroll, set an alarm, get some sleep. After all the necessary tasks have been completed, we would get an average of 75 minutes' sleep before the alarm would wake us. We had about eight minutes to get kitted up with our safety harness and personal locator beacon, put on some clothes, grab a snack and quick drink before heading out of the cabin for the next rowing shift. This would be the pattern 24 hours per day for the expected 45 days of the race. We knew that lack of sleep was the silent killer. It would gradually play havoc with our judgement and mindset and it was critical to take the opportunity for sleep whenever it was possible, no matter what was going on outside.

I lay in bed listening to the water crashing against the boat. It was getting louder and louder, more aggressive and more turbulent. It was impossible to sleep as I was being thrown around the cabin getting bumps and bruises from the bare fibreglass structure. Lady Jayne is eight metres long, 1.5 metres wide and weighs one tonne fully loaded. At that moment it struck me that we were in a tiny floating plastic bubble being tossed around at the whim of the ocean. There was nothing that we could do to improve our situation and there was absolutely no point in complaining. We had willingly chosen to be here and now we had to grin and bear it – and focus on surviving the storm.

Journal, December 13th 2019

In the cabin, boat being hammered in a storm. Weather has swung around and heavy waves hitting us on the beam. Big wind now blowing. Will and I changed heading to move forward and not get swamped, very difficult rowing. Tricky hand over to Chris and Matt. Now listening to the storm building...

... conditions now even worse. Being thrown around the cabin, boat lurching all over the place. Storm howling and water crashing against the hull. Can't believe how loud it is. Wondering how much the boat can take. Put wet gear and safety harness back on. Trying to think how to get out of the cabin if the boat starts to break up. Have to get the emergency grab bag out and into liferaft, it's 30kg and huge. Think we are about 40 miles from nearest land at El Hierro island, pitch black outside with zero visibility... Chris and Matt fighting to keep control...

I had studied structural engineering at university, and while I'm no naval architect, as I lay listening to the colossal pounding of the waves, I was beginning to wonder just how much of this constant hammering the boat could take before the hull began to fail. Suddenly there was an enormous crash and the boat lurched over. I was thrown across the cabin as the boat was struck on the side by what was likely to be more than 1,000 tonnes of water.

Out of control in the eye of the storm

There was a terrifying second of comparative silence before I heard Chris shout 'Shit, that broke my oar'. I jumped up and looked through the cabin door window to see Chris with a snapped starboard oar but Matt still rowing behind him and fighting to keep the boat stable. Five seconds later Matt shouted that his starboard oar had also snapped, caught by the next wave.

These were new carbon fibre oars designed to take tonnes of load, and they had each broken in a second. As Lady Jayne had slid sideways down the face of an enormous wave, the oar blade had been dragged down, pulled out of the hands of the rower and pushed under the boat by the surging water. The oar shaft had snapped and the rowlock mountings, made of 12-millimetre plate aluminium, had been bent at 30 degrees. The sheer power of the water was tremendous. This was now a highly dangerous situation and we needed to regain control of the boat very quickly or it could all go very wrong!

This had happened at the precise moment that Matt and Sam were about to do a changeover. Now there were three guys fighting for balance on the pitching deck of a boat which was out of control. With no oars, all forward motion had been lost, causing the autohelm to disengage and set off its screeching alarm.

The violence of the storm and turbulence of the water was thrashing our little boat around. Because we had no forward motion, the boat had swung around to be side on to the crashing waves. We were surrounded by white water rising up and down on huge swells with shrieking wind and driving rain obscuring our vision. There was a real danger that the next wave would roll the boat over. Again, that image of a capsize in the dark, in a storm, 30 miles from land, flashed through my mind. If the three rowers on deck were not properly tethered by their safety harnesses, they would be lost in seconds. There would be no way of getting them back.

We carried two spare oars and the oars for the third rowing position were lashed down on deck. As the boat pitched and tossed Sam, Matt and Chris removed the lashing and fought to replace the broken oars. There was no point in trying to leave the cabin to help the effort as there was no space on deck for anyone else and by the time Will and I had put our safety gear back on it would have been too late. With the new oars in place Sam and Chris started rowing while Matt lashed down the broken oars before heading for the cabin. Sam and Chris rowed with all of their strength and battled to gain forward movement.

The autohelm alarm was still shrieking, reminding us that it was not doing its job. It was clear that we needed to regain control of the boat as quickly as possible but this would not be possible with the autohelm connected to the tiller arm since its electronic brain was struggling to compute how to sort out a completely confused situation.

The rudder compartment was in my cabin. I opened the door, disconnected the autohelm from the tiller arm and made the mistake of grabbing the tiller with the intention of pulling it straight and correcting the rudder. It nearly pulled my arm off. It was like fighting a tiger. I was being bounced around the cabin while trying to manually straighten a large rudder which was being rammed left and right by the turbulent water. By a combination of fear-driven strength and Sam and Chris's skills on the oars we gradually brought the boat under control and reconnected the autohelm. The storm raged around us but now at least we could point Lady Jayne into the waves and reduce the immediate chances of a capsize. Then all we had to do was to ride out the storm without breaking any more important pieces of kit.

Think carefully, decide clearly

We were extremely grateful to have three experienced mariners on board who shared the rowing and through their skill managed to keep the boat stable through the worst of the storm. After six heroic hours of rowing Chris, Will and Sam needed to take a break from the battle that they had been fighting. The wind had shifted and the sea state was now more consistent but was pushing us backwards towards the start line. We didn't want to lose the distance that we had already rowed and so we deployed our para anchor. This is a small parachute which is streamed from the boat and sinks into the water to stabilise the vessel and act as a brake. It prevents the boat from being driven along by the wind. The wind was now driving us backwards and was too strong to row against. With the para anchor deployed the boat was effectively standing still. After a chaotic night we felt some relief and took the welcome opportunity to get some sleep.

At daybreak we took stock of our situation. The wind had eased and the sea was calmer but still with huge swells. We inspected the damage to the boat. The rowlocks were bent but would still work, we had brought two spare oars and the broken oars were lashed down on deck. We had not lost any important kit and our electronics all worked. We now had no spare oars but we had enough to row with. We had suffered a big fright and we quietly discussed our next move. The options were pretty stark – we were about 30 miles from the small island of El Hierro and could row there if we wanted to give up on the race, or we could adjust our plans, make do with the kit we had and row harder to make up for the time lost in the storm.

We called race control to check in and found that the four boats, including us, which had headed west and got caught by the storm were actually positioned towards the front of the race fleet. It seemed that while we had endured some hours of difficulty, it hadn't spoiled our race. At that point it really was the easiest of decisions: we would adjust as much as we needed to and keep on with our plan to break the world record. It had been a night when we had learned a lot about the Atlantic and about ourselves. We now knew what could be thrown at us but we also knew that we could deal with it. Lady Jayne had been hugely impressive and showed us what she was capable of. This made us even more determined to succeed. We had just been through hell, so now we would keep going. Our confidence was up and we intended to push harder.

8: NOTES FOR BUSINESS

I have led numerous companies through critical situations. The crisis may have been caused by internal issues such as lack of a clear strategy, poor execution or financial shortcomings. Alternatively, the business may have failed to react to changes in the marketplace, new technology or an economic downturn. At the time of writing, the world is just beginning to recover from the seismic and unexpected disruption of the global Covid-19 pandemic. This is an environmental situation that very few organisations were prepared for.

To an organisation or team in crisis, it doesn't matter what caused the problem, but rather what can be done to revitalise performance. The approach to resolving the crisis must be structured and open. The team should be made aware of the details of the situation and invited to be part of the solution to the crisis. In such situations it is normal that team members display concern. This needs to be discussed and their fears resolved. Companies which are considered to be in crisis are usually a long way away from failure. A clear plan, strong leadership and prompt action can quickly deliver very positive results and forward momentum.

It is the responsibility of the leader to own the problem. They must engage and involve the team in the cultural transition from negativity about the current difficulties into positive and committed action to build a strong future. Leaders must take responsibility for displaying and encouraging confidence in the future of the organisation.

Work with facts
There is only one true set of facts. Make sure you understand what the real position of the organisation is. Share that reality honestly and objectively. Identify leaders throughout the organisation who will promote action and who will encourage and coach others. Provide those leaders with authority and accountability.

Define the action plan – quickly

Discuss the situation openly within the entire team. Identify the key areas for action and rank them in priority order. Focus on the top 25 per cent of the key areas and define the action plan. Move rapidly to address problem areas. The target should be a stable and positive organisation within 100 days.

Communicate, communicate, communicate

Spend time communicating with the entire team – both the internal team and those external to the organisation such as suppliers or key clients. Do not be afraid to share bad news but also share details of the corrective action that you intend to take to address it. Communicate forwards by advising your team of intended actions before they hear about it from external parties or, worse, read it in the media.

Stay calm, take control

Make the progress against the plan visible and transparent. Recognise that a challenging situation allows extraordinary actions to be taken. Implement short communication lines, reduce timescales, act on priorities without delay. Be visible and open.

Challenge the organisation

Once the ship is secured demonstrate courage by inviting the team to challenge the norm and seek new approaches and processes. Take the opportunity to examine the fundamentals of the business with everything on the table for inclusion.

Invite the team on a journey

The first destination in a crisis is survival but once that is achieved the team should be invited on the next stage of the journey. That is a journey to an exciting and compelling vision of success. Discuss it, share it, believe in it.

9 SEIZE BACK THE INITIATIVE

Incredible changes will happen when you decide to take control of what you do have power over instead of craving control over what you don't.

– Steve Maraboli

The storm was a reminder of the power of the ocean and how little we could do to combat it. The result of our brief battle with the sea had been a score draw. We had been physically knocked about and, frankly, had felt more than a bit afraid, but there had been no panic. We had dealt with the situation and learned from it. We had come through it and were now more determined than ever to continue to race to the best of our ability.

We reset our planning, considering how best to manage our boat, recognising that the remaining oars especially were precious. We could not afford to lose another oar or any other equipment. We were back to our rowing schedule and had taken back control of our world as far as we could.

Understand who the real competition is

We had expected that the other rowers would be our competitive focus, but the progress of the other boats soon became a one-minute update in our daily weather routing call. In 250 million square kilometres of ocean with many weather systems and up to 1,000 kilometres between us and other rowers, we could not focus on what they were doing. We now fully appreciated that our key competitor, which was also our most dangerous one, was the ocean.

While we felt we had faced some of the worst that this key competitor could throw at us, and we had learned from the experience, we knew that we were going to need to find out a lot more. The speed at which the storm had descended on us had caught us by surprise. Dealing with the storm was a small win but we expected more storms and more challenges. It is always difficult to predict how quickly, or in what way, your competition can change its approach. We were learning to watch the ocean and to react to the rapid changes in sea state which we saw.

The expectation before we started the race was that the big waves would be our biggest challenge. But unless there is a raging storm, the ocean typically doesn't have big waves. It does, however, have huge swells. These are long, slow peaks and troughs of water which, when the wind is blowing, will be capped by white-capped breakers which will roll over the swells. There is little that can prepare you for the sheer scale of the walls of water all around you. The swells could be immense and in the early days of the crossing presented an ominous visual reminder of what we were facing. Sitting rowing on Lady Jayne was like sitting in a bathtub on the centre spot of Manchester United's Old Trafford pitch looking up at the stadium all around, except the encircling structure wouldn't be terraces of seats and high roofs; it would be billions of tonnes of water. Scary! While it was intimidating, our boat had been designed by Rannoch for exactly this situation and she was remarkably stable. As the swells swept in, one behind the other, Lady Jayne would rise over the massive surge of water and settle down the far side. We felt as if a massive invisible hand was lifting us towards the sky before lowering us into a valley on the other side of a mountain. It was like rowing on a roller coaster.

Journal, December 14th 2019

Satellite phone message from investor colleague. Conservatives won the election. Labour's threat of free broadband for everyone gone away (crazy idea, who would pay to build the networks?). New institutional funding, on hold pending the election result, paid into ITS Technology today. Huge relief! Finance and weather improving. Now just row!

The more aggressive competition were the waves we called growlers. These were smaller breakers, about one metre high and whipped up by the wind, which would break all around us. At night, rowing without lights to save night vision, we would get no warning before a tonne of water would break over us unexpectedly from apparently any direction. Arriving with a sudden rush and roar, the growlers could knock a rower off balance, out of their seat or, worse, out of the boat. If we didn't stay focused on securely closing the cabin door each and every time we passed through it, a growler could rush in soaking everything inside, including electrical gear. If it was a big enough growler, it could fill the cabin with water, destabilise the boat and potentially end our race.

We began to understand the way the ocean behaved and realised that if we worked with it, instead of trying to fight it (a hopeless task!) it could actually help us to go faster. Each day we made good progress was another victory over the competition.

Take control of your surroundings

While we could not control the ocean, we could control how we reacted to it. Dealing with the waves and currents was a learning experience. We slowly discovered how best to benefit from the energy of the wind and direction of the waves.

Some reactions, though, were unplanned. In the early part of the race our three experienced mariners had some days of suffering badly from seasickness. In such a tight space there is simply no room for polite discretion and it is difficult to move quickly from lying in the cabin to leaning over the gunwales. Despite everyone's best efforts, the deck was occasionally splattered. It was unpleasant for the rowers but the constant wash of seawater over the row deck soon rinsed the mess away. It was worse for those feeling unwell as their rowing, sleeping and eating were compromised, yet they were still expected to complete their shifts on the oars.

The sea state could change by the hour and the direction of the wind and waves would determine our entire day. The number of miles covered, relatively comfortable or very difficult rowing, easy sleep or none were all dictated by the sea's state. Our ideal was a rolling sea with wind from the east as that would lift the boat and push us along. Windless days with flat calm seas were not welcome as it meant that we had to row hard for every single metre. Turbulent and extremely windy days would challenge us in other ways. Some days the rain was so hard that the only way we could keep our eyes open while rowing was to wear swimming goggles. Even then, apart from thin windproof smocks, we didn't bother with foul weather gear – a pile of sodden clothing was an unwelcome bed partner in a small, crowded cabin. It was very heavy to row in, was impossible to dry and one way or another would slow the boat. We shivered through the worst weather, staying warm by rowing harder (another one per cent saved).

Regular hot meals were a welcome luxury and key to maintaining energy and morale. Our food was a selection of high-calorie freeze-dried expedition meals, reconstituted with water heated over a Jetboil. The choices were good and included spaghetti bolognese, chilli con carne, curry and stew, including vegetarian options, pasta and muesli. This was supplemented by a dip into the daily goodie bag of chocolate, nuts or other snacks (see also page 63). All of this was washed down with water, water and more water. Making a hot drink required the luxury of time and ideally a calm sea. Both of which were in very short supply.

The shower was a sports drink bottle full of (cold) desalinated water squirted slowly over your head and washed all around with soap while trying to maintain balance standing on a slippery moving deck. After a tough rowing shift this was considered to be a luxury.

The toilet was a bucket, also prone to sliding around on a rolling deck, in full view of the rest of the crew. During what could be described on some days as a monotonous regime, the filling and then emptying of the bucket over the side of a pitching boat became a suitably distracting subject of amused discussion – as long as you were the rower furthest away from the bucket holder as it was emptied!

Nourishment, cleanliness and sleep were the holy trinity of maintaining a healthy rower. Once the nourishment and cleaning routines were finished our average sleep period was 75 minutes before getting back on the oars for another 120-minute shift. Repeat. Repeat.

We learned how to adapt our rowing to the environment and our boat management and personal care also improved daily. We focused on getting the boat and the processes to operate with a rhythm, efficiently and smoothly. This added to our ability to concentrate the majority of our effort on rowing and on making the boat go faster.

Interrogate the operation for marginal gains

If a process can improve in effectiveness by one per cent each day for 365 days, the cumulative gain will be 1.01^{365}, which is a factor of 37. That means that the process would be 37 times better than when it started. Compound improvements are hugely powerful and we knew that we could not out-row, but we could outperform. We were therefore looking for incremental gains in every part of the operation of the boat with the intention of achieving a large cumulative improvement.

We started with the highest priority areas. As a team of five rowers, we had trained hard. Chris, Sam and Will had more marine experience and a more efficient rowing technique but every one of us was prepared to give it our absolute best. The efficiency of the rowing was critical because the biggest opportunities for substantial improvement in our performance were in the power we applied to the propulsion of the boat. We were each rowing as hard as we possibly could while taking advantage of every puff of wind and push of current that we could interpret from our daily weather bulletin.

We found different ways to drive ourselves on with different targets: each row shift would set a target of miles covered for the next shift to beat, or would do sprint rowing where we would row absolutely flat out for 20 strokes, then row 20 regular strokes before sprinting again, each crew watching the speedometer to compare the maximum speed achieved. The fastest speed briefly achieved was almost 8 knots – but that was down the face of a wave with a following wind! These approaches will have improved our average speed a little but they were not sustainable over the long term.

The next question was: if we couldn't row harder, could we row for longer? We knew from our own experience, and that of other crews, that two hours on followed by two hours off was considered optimal in maintaining the stroke rate and boat speed. Where we could make a difference was at the changeover. We changed rowers every two hours, which meant 12 changes per day. We knew that many crews would use the changeover to perform small tasks or grab some snacks, take a drink, have a pee or just have a chat. That could easily mean a five- or ten-minute gap between rowing. If that is repeated at every changeover, ten minutes x 12 changes = 120 minutes, or two hours of non-rowing per day. Over 40 days that would be 80 hours, or 3.3 days. On a good day we were covering 80–100 miles so that could be 300 miles-plus of progress lost, which is ten per cent of the total distance!

We worked hard to have less than 30 seconds' break between rowers, ideally less than 15. This meant thinking through the changeover process and choreographing the exit and entry from the rowing seat. We made sure that the seat position and cushion were acceptable to both rowers, that drinks bottles were filled and pocket snacks were in place, that the rower was clipped onto the safety line and that sun cream, clothes, glasses, hats and gloves were all on before the rower sat down so that he was immediately ready to row.

On Christmas Day you would normally expect to have a break and some celebration, but it was a good rowing day and so we didn't stop. Not a single minute's break. In our imagination all of the other boats would have stopped rowing for a break and a call to families. That meant we gained one more hour of rowing input than most boats; that was three miles or 0.1 per cent gain. Every bit counts.

Don't forget to enjoy the rainbows

Rowing across an ocean is best described as plain hard work. It is a case of sheer will and determination and the ability to just keeping going when your body hurts all over and your brain is screaming for a rest. The climate we were conducting this routine in was harsh. In each 24 hours we could experience the extremes of wind, waves, sun and thunderous squalls when it would rain so hard that it flattened the ocean and we were forced to wear swimming goggles to see where we were going as we kept rowing. The physical assault pounded our bodies, while the lack of sleep scrambled our brains, at times causing hallucinations and short periods of confusion.

But in so many ways, it was also an extraordinary, wonderful, life-enhancing experience. The view from the boat was predictable, comprising 50 per cent ocean and 50 per cent sky. While both were always visible, neither looked the same for more than a few minutes. The colour of the sea would continuously change, with waves and swells coming and going. When the sun shone and the wind blew, the waves crashed around us with sapphire blue and white water sweeping past the boat and glittering in the reflected sunlight. An hour later the sun could be hidden and a brisk wind would sculpt the water into dark, sharp spikes which reminded me of granite on some of the mountains I have climbed.

Sea life would come and go at its own pace. We saw whales as they surfaced for air, and on one occasion a large shark surfed down the face of a rolling wave alongside us. Dolphins and porpoises were frequent visitors with pods of up to 30 members happily swimming around us. We saw numerous turtles which would gently slide beneath the surface as we approached. Each night we were bombarded by flying fish, which would glide over the boat. At 25 centimetres long and weighing 0.5 kg they could fly for up to 100 metres at 40 kilometres per hour and it was a shock if one hit you. They would zoom out of the dark, flying over us and around us; occasionally one would hit us or the boat before it dropped onto the deck, at which point we would briefly pause rowing to catch it and return it to the water.

Journal, December 22nd 2019

Lack of sleep literally driving me crazy. Convinced that my daughter was sitting next to me chatting as I was rowing. Will was laughing and taking the mickey! Woke up for my next shift wondering which harbour we were going to go into to change rowers (there are no harbours mid Atlantic). Completely weird dreams. Never hallucinated before, feel as if I am operating in a daze... need to find a way to sleep more, even another 15 minutes each break.

Above us the sky was another changing world. Whether deep blue clear days or massive bubbling storm clouds bringing heavy weather, there was always something new and beautiful to watch. It was the night sky, though, which was the most memorable. One night as we rowed we watched the incredible colours of a lunar rainbow (moonbow) dance around the full moon. Since in the mid-Atlantic we were 1,500 miles from shore, we didn't suffer from light pollution and we were able to enjoy views of the Milky Way and innumerable galaxies of stars as we had never seen them before. The brightness of the stars and their contrast against the deepest black of the night sky was extraordinary. Matt, our resident astronomer, pointed out the planets and constellations and demonstrated how mariners in ancient times would navigate by the cosmos. We watched the International Space Station traverse across our route many times and realised that its crew, at a height of 250 miles, were probably the closest living people in the universe to us. We imagined they were looking down on us as we were looking up at them.

It was an extreme environment but nobody had forced us to be where we were. We had chosen to be in the race and we considered ourselves to be the luckiest guys in the world doing something we loved, surrounded by an astonishing landscape each moment of every day. We reminded ourselves to soak it up and enjoy every minute of it – even the rainy ones.

Sometimes you just have to celebrate

By New Year's Eve we had been rowing for 19 days. Except for the few hours when we sheltered from the storm, we hadn't taken a moment's break. Since we were somewhere in the mid-Atlantic and in no specific time zone, we could celebrate the start of the new year whenever we wanted to. It was a beautiful day with excellent sea conditions and so we kept rowing on. In the middle of the day, as we were about to change rowers, skipper Chris called a break. He announced a 30-minute rest and we took a short time to jointly celebrate Christmas and New Year.

We spread ourselves as comfortably as possible around the tiny row deck and took out the bag of Christmas goodies that we had packed in anticipation of this lunch. We had brought some small gifts, including the obligatory Terry's Chocolate Oranges and we each popped on our red Christmas hats while Chef Matt prepared a lunch for everyone. In honour of Santa and his sleigh, he served a freeze-dried portion of reindeer stew, while vegetarian Sam enjoyed a festive three (wise) bean chilli. With the intention of raising a toast to the race sponsors we had even packed a half litre of Talisker Whisky. Strangely, after three weeks at sea drinking only water, nobody wanted to touch it.

Unbeknown to any of us, Chris had quietly arranged for our families to write personal letters and cards for us to open on Christmas Day. He brought them out of his kitbag and handed them around. The letters were opened and read out loud so that they could be shared and enjoyed by the entire crew. The messages, all of them inspiring and encouraging, with the odd joke thrown in, felt very special and welcome in our remote and intimate world. We had been away from our families and loved ones for weeks and our bodies and minds had been pummelled by the sea and the sheer physical effort of non-stop rowing. Our emotional barriers were lowered as we took these quiet moments to reflect on the love and support which was following us across the ocean.

Sam was intending to propose to his girlfriend as soon as we landed in Antigua. Everyone except his girlfriend knew of his plans. His letter from his mum was very special. It celebrated with beautiful words his journey from childhood to this imminent engagement milestone in his life. Sam started to read it out loud but soon couldn't see through the tears and it took three of us to finish it as one after another choked with emotion. Five guys sitting sobbing and laughing in the middle of the Atlantic wasn't exactly how we had expected ourselves to behave. It didn't matter; it just brought us closer as a team.

Thirty minutes over, Chris called time and we were back on the oars.

Merry Christmas, Happy New Year.

9: NOTES FOR BUSINESS

The strategic review of any enterprise should not be reserved only for times of trouble. Successful leaders regularly take time out of the organisation to determine how best to reset and rebuild, even when the business is performing well. Such a review will sharpen the focus, boost corporate performance and inspire the team when the market is mostly occupied by competitive organisations which are thinking only of short-term results.

A leadership team must give itself permission to turn off the autopilot and prevent the organisation progressing the way it has always done. This allows consideration to be given to the overall performance and health of the enterprise as well as the freedom to consider where their business will fit into the future. The result of this free thinking is the ability to seize the initiative, resolve current or historical threats and benefit from new opportunities. Frequently organisations recognise that the biggest threat they face is not the challenge of change, but resistance to change.

Properly used, a process of review will suggest simple changes in perspective, which in turn provide the opportunity to explore powerful outcomes. By carefully considering the future, the organisation can develop the ability at all levels to think and adapt to external forces and internal opportunities. A clear idea of future possibilities allows leaders to maintain agility and mitigate risk in the case of external threats.

Stay in control
At all times maintain a position of clear objectivity with the organisation. Be prepared at all times to examine the fundamentals of the operation with everything on the table for consideration. Base decisions on the overall goal of the organisation. Make the decision criteria transparent.

Don't get caught by surprise

Constantly scan the market, competition and client base to identify changes and trends. Check positive trends against your vision of success. Is it helpful? Should you integrate it into your planning? Explore how each potential negative trend can be interpreted to provide a positive opportunity to develop. Maintain an open mind, be curious and explore similar or parallel sectors for ideas and new initiatives.

Consider external threats to build resilience

Recognise that facing and addressing threats are part of developing a world-class organisation. Record and celebrate where potential threats have been overcome and turned to your advantage. Communication of the organisation's positive result against a challenge will encourage the team to recognise their own strength and capability.

Do not fight the competition

Begin with the client's requirements and work back from there. What is it that the client values? What are they prepared to pay for? Only once that is fully understood should your product or service be developed or refined. Do not focus development of your organisation on chasing 'market share' or beating competitors. Rather look for 'opportunity share' and the chance to offer valued products and services into areas that other players are not considering.

Feedback is golden

Enjoy constructive feedback. Build mechanisms to encourage open thinking and open communication. Recognise that feedback of disappointment is always an opportunity to improve the operations and enhance and deepen the client relationship. Don't forget that suppliers and business partners are clients as well. How you can help them? What are their concerns? What would they want you to do differently?

Get better and bigger will come

Do not focus the operation on short-term financial results. Ensure that the emphasis is on building excellence in products, services and operations. A one per cent improvement every day for one year will deliver a system or process which is 37 times better at the end of the period. This improvement will impress and retain clients or partners.

10 DON'T EVER GET COMPLACENT

Keep hoping for the best, be prepared for the worst, and don't be surprised by anything in between.

– Maya Angelou

Maintaining a positive mindset is critical to all aspects of performance. This is especially true in endurance sport where every day can be very much like the previous day except that each part of your body hurts a bit more.

Nobody had forced us to be in the middle of the Atlantic in a small rowing boat. We were all there willingly and we knew what to expect. Matt described the idea of the race when we first discussed it as 'pain, pain, and more pain – and hope that you don't die'. But, as the saying goes, pain is just the French word for bread – so eat it up and keep going. We knew the target, we had planned, planned and replanned our approach to the race and now it was a reality.

Oceans do not take prisoners

We anticipated that it would be tough but we were still not fully prepared for the absolute battering that our bodies and minds would take. The physical stress of continuous rowing was very challenging. Pain was a constant. It was only a matter of where and how much. Muscles ached and hands, feet and bottoms were rubbed raw through contact with the oars, footplate and seat. Rowing hand grips, which would last a year on an indoor rowing machine, were shredded after five days. Foot straps and heel grips rubbed the skin away and caused blisters, which in turn rubbed away until feet looked like an infected, bloody mess.

Seat cushion choice (we had taken a variety) became an art. The choice for your next shift depended on which part of your backside was the most painful at that particular time. We wiped our bottom cheeks with alcohol and dusted ourselves with talcum powder to dry the skin and help recovery but by the third week just sitting on the rowing seat was agony.

In addition to physical discomfort there was the continuous pressure of dealing with the ocean; rough days, calm days, big seas, headwinds, torrential rain, cold, hot, blistering sun – potentially all within a 24-hour period. Observing the sea state, anticipating dangerous waves, monitoring navigation and keeping watch for approaching ships meant that we had to focus and concentrate at all times. There was no time for relaxation.

Sleeeeep....

One of the biggest challenges was dealing with the lack of sleep. We were able to get a maximum of 75–80 minutes' sleep in any one rest period. The natural sleep cycle averages 90 minutes and a person sleeping overnight would normally go through four or five sleep cycles which together provide quality rest. Because we were never able to sleep through even one complete cycle our brains never fully rested. Over a period of days this drains away energy reserves and plays havoc with cognitive skills. Routine activities become challenging. Midnight rowing changeovers involved moving from the cabin back to the rowing seat, passing a crewmate on a pitching boat, in complete darkness and potentially in lashing rain while surrounded by a roiling sea. In normal circumstances this needed great care. In a sleep-deprived state these situations can become very dangerous. Regular conditions can appear confusing and even making an everyday decision can become complicated.

In the repetitive world of row, eat, sleep, repeat, time becomes abstract: an example is coming off shift, getting into the cabin and falling dead asleep in the middle of removing your rowing kit and safety harness. Then waking up with a shock, wondering where you are and realising that you are half dressed, assuming that you must have been dressing for your row shift, putting your rowing and safety kit on and calling to the guys on deck to say that you are ready when they are... to be told that you only went off shift 35 minutes ago! OK, get undressed again. Get some food, set an alarm for 45 minutes, get a bit more sleep.

Occasionally the confusion had a humorous side as the steady rhythm of rowing combined with sleep deprivation lulls the brain into playing strange tricks. Hallucinations were quite frequent (see the journal entry on page 101). One time, through the veil of partial sleep, shapes and shadows in the water began to look like familiar objects. I was convinced that I knew precisely where we were because I could see Tesco in the distance!

Tough times don't last – tough teams do

We had been together as a team for almost three years and had got to know each other pretty well. Each of us had been through our own challenges in life. Between us we had faced rough times at sea, difficult weeks on extreme expeditions, competition at the highest levels in sport, business crises and personal loss. We had discussed these experiences and got to understand each other and how we would each be likely to behave in a demanding or dangerous situation. Through every difficulty we had faced together, we had maintained a positive outlook. Despite some very difficult days and extremely tough conditions both in training and in the race, there had never once been a complaint or argument within the team.

We knew each other's strengths and weaknesses. We trusted each other. We were all committed to achieving the same goal and were fully aware that we would have to work together to deliver it. We never forgot that the agreed motto in the team was 'Be kind'. We worked well through the good days but we knew that we would each have bad days and we were determined that we would support each other through those difficult periods no matter how tough they were. Maintaining such a positive mindset was worth at least another one per cent.

The storm on the first day had been a shock to our system but we had survived it and we knew that we were now stronger as a result of it. Our toughest day of physical exertion had been making three miles of progress after 24 hours of grinding rowing into a headwind. Not one word of complaint was spoken. Everyone dug deep and did their job. The daily challenge of driving the boat as fast as we could had become routine.

Our best day of progress had been over 100 miles. We passed the halfway point with a small cheer and a smile. We were 1,500 miles away from land in any direction and we were a happy but tired crew bobbing about on a tiny boat in the middle of a vast ocean. Only half of the distance left to row – it was all downhill from here!

Journal, December 27th 2019

Off shift, 4am, feeling very wet and cold. Eating minestrone soup and Christmas cake — perfect snack. Last 2 hours was hard. Visibility max 10 metres, beyond 5 metres could only see shapes. Waves from all directions. Big ones about 3 to 4 metres with white tops knocking us about and looking like angry bears with open mouths attacking from above. Smaller growlers, like hungry crocodiles rushing at us. Strange what rain, lack of visibility and tiredness turn the shapes into. Hands sore, bum cheeks sore, heel very sore. Living the dream.

We recognised that the ocean was another world to that which we regularly inhabited. The climate and scenery could be beautiful and mysteriously calming before very quickly transforming itself into something which was brutal and deadly. The wind and waves tested us endlessly but we were becoming familiar with the changing nature of the sea state. We were comfortable in what we were doing and we were relaxing into it as we began to feel that we were in command of the situation. The ocean environment had become our normal and we were getting increasingly familiar with the temperamental nature of the world that surrounded us. Our belief was growing that we knew how to handle it, but as we were about to find out, that was a major case of overconfidence.

Don't confuse confidence with control

The sea state could change completely within 15 minutes. From flowing swells which pushed us forwards, to breaking peaks which would throw us around and make rowing very uncomfortable and difficult. Our increased confidence meant that now we didn't even notice some of the larger waves which had intimidated us in the first week.

Some days it looked and felt as if we were trying to navigate through small but continuously moving canyons with vertical walls. We would rush down the face of the swell before struggling to rise up the opposite wall of crashing water. Going up the face of an oncoming wave, the 20 metres of near-vertical surging water would slow us to an almost stop. As the wave crested, the front of the boat would be lifted upwards at an angle of 45 degrees or more and we would be looking down over the stern of the boat into a valley of water. We would row hard to reach the summit of the wave and get the boat level before the next wave arrived.

On a few occasions, while rising from the deep trough of water between massive swells, the boat was caught with the bow pushed so far upwards that she was nearly vertical and in danger of pitchpoling backwards onto the crew. At that point one of the crew would quickly jump to the side of the boat, causing her to slew across the face of the wave and slide back down into the valley. All very exciting for a few minutes as we regrouped and started rowing again. While the sea state and weather were completely outside our control, we were increasingly impressed with Lady Jayne and just how assured she was in heavy seas. Our confidence in our ability to handle her whatever the weather was growing ever stronger. We were relaxing into the journey and believing we had it all under control. How wrong we were.

And then the world turned upside down

On a blustery day with a brisk wind and helpful following swells, Sam, Matt and I were rowing and confident of making good progress on our shift. The swells were getting bigger, coming from behind, lifting us and surfing the boat forwards – wow, this was fun! We whooped each time we were pushed forwards, appreciating the help being given to us by the sheer power of the water. We were enjoying the ride as the swells continued to build, but we noticed that the direction of the waves was becoming more confused with water striking us on both the stern and beam.

That made the rowing more challenging but it was no problem, we were in control and we were flying along. Suddenly the stern of the boat was lifted by a huge surge of water just as another wave struck the side. Lady Jayne was flipped over and capsized. We were all flung from the boat, thrown high over the side safety lines. As we reached the end of the tethers fixed to our harnesses we dropped into the water.

My first thought was, 'Oh good, this water is warmer than I expected.' I was about two metres underwater as I looked to my left and was relieved to see Matt beginning to swim towards the surface. As I looked up I could see Lady Jayne upturned in front of me. By the time Matt and I surfaced, Lady Jayne was lying on her side and Sam was already scrambling onto the upturned hull.

Our precious oars were flailing around in the water with waves continuing to break over us and over the boat. Having broken two oars on our first night, we had no further spares and if the oars we were using were dragged under the boat, they could have been snapped by the rolling waves. Matt and I stayed in the foaming water doing all we could to protect the oars while Sam climbed across the boat and used his weight to help her to right. As she slowly rolled over, we could see

Chris and Will looking out through the windows in their cabin doors. They were wondering what had just happened as their world of sleep had turned upside down and their bed had relocated to the cabin ceiling. As Sam straightened out the kit on deck, Matt and I secured the oars and climbed back on board.

We checked the boat for damage. Everything on the row deck was secured with lanyards. We had lost a drinking bottle and a seat cushion where the fixings between shift changes had been overlooked. As we watched the wind and current rapidly wash the cushion and bottle away, we saw just how quickly an untethered rower would have been lost. The chances of us being able to row fast enough to recover somebody who had fallen overboard without a safety line were very, very slim. We remembered Ian Couch's words of 'always, always, always be tied on'. His determination that we take his directive seriously took on a whole new meaning in the sharp reality of the current situation.

January 2nd 2020

Just finished capsizing the boat. Ha ha…! Big wave up the stern lifted Lady Jayne out of the water then a wave on the side knocked us over. Sam, Matt and I suddenly swimming. Water wasn't too cold. Lady Jayne took it in her stride and slowly rolled the right way up again. Climbed back on board, no one hurt. Lost a few bits of kit. The speed they disappeared in the wind and current was scary! No harm done, laughing about it now but could have been a very different story if we weren't tethered to the boat… Happy New Year!

With the boat once again the right way up, Chris and Will could return to their beds. Sam, Matt and I checked the boat over, put everything back in place and returned to rowing. It had been 15 minutes of excitement and drama which we would laugh about later but right then it meant we had 15 minutes of non-rowing to make up for!

Never again did we allow ourselves the misguided luxury of believing that we were fully in control of our environment.

10: NOTES FOR BUSINESS

Creating a successful organisation or building a world-class team is never straightforward. The world in which we all operate is neither consistent nor predictable. The most successful leaders recognise that flexibility and the ability to react quickly to an uncertain situation is key to achieving success.

Challenges are opportunities for growth. Change is an opportunity to improve and develop. Do not allow your team to see change as something to fear. Address the fear by discussing with the team the new status that the organisation is striving for. Carefully evaluate the opportunities and the shifts in the marketplace and make sure that you deal only in facts. Share your excitement by being enthusiastic about the freedom to make real and substantial change. Encourage the team to visualise for themselves what could be possible within their area of responsibility or the organisation as a whole.

Make heroes of the high-performing teams by praising their approach to a challenge. If high performers are encouraged, they will run with the opportunity. Frequently, when the boundaries are removed, a high-performing team will positively surprise themselves with what they can achieve.

Tough times don't last...
... but tough teams do. Deal with any crisis as it arrives but spend more time and energy thinking about driving changes that last and are aligned to the vision of success. Build belief by measuring and communicating progress of which the team is proud. They will then own it and deliver it.

Thoughts determine actions

Thoughts create feelings, which promote actions, which drives results. Consider the culture that you wish to develop within the team and ensure it is challenging but positive. Ensure that the culture is inclusive and positive. Win hearts, and minds will follow.

If making difficult decisions – move fast

When facing a difficult situation consider the options carefully and logically and then act quickly. Move boldly and decisively; learn quickly. Do not be afraid to make a mistake. Not acting is the biggest mistake. If it goes wrong explore the reasons why. Learn from the experience.

Stay flexible – agility allows rapid take-up of opportunity or response to adversity

If everything is under control then you are not moving fast enough. A degree of instability will maintain agility and flexibility within the organisation. Do not build expensive structures of people, systems or hardware in any part of the organisation. Be ready to quickly pull a structure down and rebuild it in a new configuration. Move before you are forced to move.

Do not react to every shift in the market

Some trends are short term and will not lead to lasting market change. Assess each market trend carefully but do not be afraid not to react. Maintain the focus on longer-term goals.

Be optimistic – positive energy is contagious

Always set a positive example; be approachable, consistent and open. Make champions visible. Positive thoughts and actions create belief and generate energy which transfers to others.

11 SEE THE INVISIBLE

The difference between being ordinary and extraordinary is doing the right thing while nobody is watching.

– Jim Rohn

I believe that ordinary people can achieve extraordinary results. With a clear vision of success and an inspired culture, a team can be greater than the sum of the parts. Such a team can achieve goals which individual members of the team may never have aspired to. I define this approach with the simple words Commit, Connect, Create:

- ➡ **Commit** to a clear and agreed vision of success. Share it.
- ➡ **Connect** everyone to the goal. Have a simple, visible and focused plan.
- ➡ **Create** a team. Build a culture where everyone is inspired to deliver their best.

By definition, extraordinary results mean results which are substantially better than those normally expected. It means understanding what the best is, and then exceeding it.

Somebody has to be the best

We knew what the best was. The previous world record for a five-man crew on the route we were following was set by the Nauti Buoys at 36 days, 19 hrs and 9 mins. They had set the goal and were, by definition, the best. So, we knew what our vision of success was: any time less than 36 days, 19 hrs and 9 mins for rowing across the Atlantic from La Gomera, Spain to English Harbour, Antigua. We had our goal and had committed to it. We had created our plan to achieve the goal, it was visible and we were focused on delivering it.

We had created a team which was far wider than the five of us in the boat. Our friends and families provided critical encouragement, our sponsors generously supported our cause and experts like Stokey, Charlie Pitcher and Angus Collins had provided specialist advice. Members of our families had taken key roles in marketing and sponsorship fundraising. We had spoken to audiences at schools, conferences, business clubs and completed interviews with the radio, TV and press. We had reached a broader audience than we ever imagined and we considered them all to be members of the Ocean5 family. We were extremely grateful to everyone who had become involved in the Ocean5 project and who would contribute, in any way, to helping the Plastic Soup Foundation to remove plastics from the earth's oceans. But to deliver our vision of success, which was to be the fastest or best five-man crew ever to row across the Atlantic, meant that we had to deliver as a crew of rowers.

Take a step back

Each day at sea we dealt with whatever the ocean threw at us. Our world was a four-metre row deck, three rowing seats and two tiny cabins. We had survived the storm and dealt with the capsize. These experiences had shown us, clearly and brutally, that we weren't the masters of the environment we were in, but we felt that we were becoming masters of our boat. We were proud that we had continuously improved, smoothed and adapted the boat activities to make the days and nights as efficient and comfortable as possible. Five rowers and Lady Jayne had become one team.

Together we had created an effective rhythm: row, eat, sleep, make water, maintain boat, toilet, wash, repeat. Within that continual routine, distractions were welcome, whether repairing a piece of equipment or something more demanding. Every couple of weeks we would dive into the ocean to scrape off the slime, weed, barnacles and other creatures that grew on the hull of the boat and slowed it down. This was fun but also disconcerting as we were in water with an average depth of 8,000 metres and had no idea what was swimming around us. We had seen numerous sharks and jellyfish and we knew that a number of ocean rowing boats had been attacked by large marlin which had impaled the boat with their sharp bills. With one crew member acting as lookout for inquisitive sharks, we took the chance to enjoy the unusual experience of swimming completely alone in the middle of the Atlantic.

It was easy to get lost in the total magnificence of the ocean environment but if we were to achieve our goal, it was important to remember that we were in a race. We had seen and spoken to a few commercial vessels which had come close to us, but we had not seen another rowing boat since an hour after we left Spain. We were given our position in the race each day during our weather routing call and information was also sent via satellite phone messages from family and friends. We knew the progress we were making and that of our competitors. Each time we received new information that another crew had covered more miles than us over the previous 24 hours, or was closing the gap to us, it gave us the urge to row harder, to make marginal changes to our rowing system and challenge ourselves to find another 0.1 knots of boat speed.

Sometimes, in order to improve your performance, you do need to take a dispassionate look at the overall situation. In a field of 36 boats, we were lying fourth in the race and leading our five-man class. Ahead of us were two crews of four rowers and one of three. The Fortitude IV and Rowed Less Travelled four-man crews were both well organised, strong crews and good guys. The BROAR crew was three Scottish brothers who were strong and fit and highly competent mariners. All were in Rannoch 45 boats, the same as our Lady Jayne. This is a boat designed to be optimal for a four-person crew. We were a five-man crew and therefore our boat carried about 200 kg of extra weight comprising the fifth rower and his kit, food, water, heavier life raft, etc. While we offset that extra weight by having a fifth rower, with wind and weather effects it wasn't a balanced equation.

Journal, January 7th 2020

Fantastic day – saw dolphin, 2 whales (or the same one twice, Minke I think) and a turtle. Following sea and wind pushing us along. Over 100 miles rowed in 24 hours. Just what we needed after a few days of tough conditions. Staying ahead of 'Row for veterans' and catching 'Broar'. Everyone smiling... now need some food, and sleep...

Each time the weather was calm, our five-man rowing system would close the gap to the boats in front of us. But every time the fleet got a boost from the wind, we would receive updates telling us that the lighter boats were pushed forwards faster and the gap would open again. Since we were now in the trade winds, the east to west weather systems were predominant and catching the lighter boats became a daily frustration.

Accept that it isn't easy

Our race plan had been to divide the crossing into three phases of 1,000 miles each. We planned to treat the first phase as a sprint and to row as fast as we absolutely could. Research of previous results told us that the boat which was leading at 1,000 miles was frequently the winning boat at 3,000 miles. We had been fourth at 1,000 miles.

We had planned that for the second 1,000-mile phase we would concentrate on efficiency of rowing and maintaining our health and fitness. We were at the end of that second phase and had allowed ourselves to settle into a regime that reflected the state of the crew. Physical damage was showing up in all areas: hands, feet and buttocks were extremely sore with blisters and infection, we had each lost a lot of body weight; and exhaustion felt like a constant state. The overnight sessions had begun to feel more challenging. The moon was no longer lighting up the ocean and the dark nights and frequent heavy squalls threatened to dampen spirits. It was noticeable that conversation had dropped off and each rower retreated into his thoughts, wishing the two-hour shift in the cold and dark would pass as quickly as possible. There was even a question of whether we should just accept our position in the race and take it easy for the last 1,000 miles. We discussed this briefly and just as briefly we dismissed it. We may have been tired and our bodies may have been hurting, but we came to race and we would keep racing until we crossed the finish line.

We had trained individually and together as a crew for many months before we started the race. We felt that we had trained hard and had focused on both strength and stamina. Being at sea soon showed us, though, that our training was not adequate preparation for the scale of challenge that an ocean crossing presents. The operating environment was more difficult, the sea more unpredictable, the physical effort greater and the strain on our bodies through lack of sleep and injuries more painful than we had anticipated. Yet, to become the best we had to continue to drive ourselves on. We needed to push harder and find the further areas of improvement which we felt were still there to be grabbed even though we couldn't easily see them. Challenging the best means finding an extra one per cent of performance, again and again. Over 35 days, which was our targeted time, one per cent improvement per day, every day, would yield around a 40 per cent overall improvement in performance. We needed to find more of that 40 per cent.

Making continuous progress meant finding more areas and processes that we could improve. But we had already made so many improvements that further opportunities appeared to be invisible. We would only find them if we stayed sharp (easier said than done after minimal sleep), interrogated the boat and continuously challenged our own performance. To achieve this, it was critical that we maintained a competitive mindset, took a step back and questioned everything we were doing. We could not be afraid to change things around, with the single objective of making the boat go faster. We knew that we had to sacrifice anything that did not contribute to a fast finish but we also knew that we were very tired.

Ten words changed our world

We moved into the third phase of 1,000 miles determined to accelerate our speed towards Antigua. Having agreed

Sam's thousand-yard stare of sleep exhaustion

Chris showing the effect of days and nights of insufficient sleep

Grabbing a short sleep whenever possible

Despite cramped conditions, Matt and Sam enjoy a break

Matt prepared a medical kit for most eventualities

Injuries were caused by friction to hands, feet and backsides

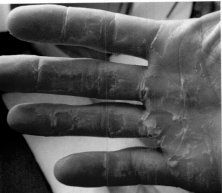

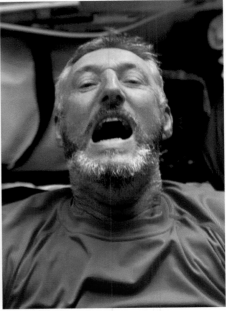

Infected blisters in foot straps made rowing painful

Supergluing a broken tooth back in – it didn't work!

Will boiling water, filling flasks
and rehydrating meal pouches

Sam taking a drinking bottle
shower while Will and I row

Matt resting off shift.
This cabin needed to
hold 3 rowers at once

Rotas, charts, emergency
checklists, radio call signs, all
designed to help fuzzy minds.
Boat is marked with sides
1 and 2 so that in a capsize
those trapped inside know
which way others are
rolling the boat upright

Celebrating Christmas and New Year for 30 minutes was
our first rowing break for 19 days

Flares and celebration after crossing the finish line in English Harbour, Antigua

Just in case we weren't sure!

The new world record time

THE CREW – BEFORE AND AFTER
Clockwise from top left:

Sam Coxon
Kevin Gaskell
Matt Gaskell
Chris Hodgson
Will Hollingshead

WORLD RECORD

THIS CERTIFICATE IS PROUDLY PRESENTED TO

THE OCEAN 5

Kevin Gaskell, Matt Gaskell, Will Hollingshead, Chris Hodgson & Sam Coxon

who rowed the boat Lady Jayne across the Atlantic Ocean in the Talisker Whisky Atlantic Challenge 2019 from San Sebastian de La Gomera, Canary Islands on 12 December 2019 to Nelsons Dockyard, Antigua on 17 January 2020 with a time of 35 Days 19 Hours 50 Minutes to become the

FASTEST TEAM OF FIVE TO ROW FROM LA GOMERA TO ANTIGUA

ISSUED: *18th September 2021*

CERTIFICATE

The fastest crossing of the Atlantic east to west on the Trade Winds I route by a team of five is 35 days 19 hr 50 min by The Ocean5 – Kevin Gaskell, Matt Gaskell, Will Hollingshead, Chris Hodgson and Sam Coxon (all UK) – who rowed from San Sebastian in Spain to English Harbour in Antigua between 12 December 2019 and 17 January 2020 on board *Lady Jayne*.

OFFICIALLY AMAZING

WWW.GUINNESSWORLDRECORDS.COM

Guinness World Record certificate

that everything possible should be done to row as quickly as possible we made further changes. Since we had already choreographed our rowing changeovers to maximise rowing time, we tried reducing the number of times we would take on calorific snacks and water during the rowing shifts. We agreed that a quick bite of a snack or gulp of water was now only allowed every 20 minutes, but 30 minutes was better. We tried to reduce the frequency of toilet breaks, but that could potentially end in a mess and wasn't considered to be the most effective approach. We felt that we were trying everything to go faster but we were nibbling at the edges and fatigue was taking its toll. We needed to think bigger.

Each boat in the race carries a Yellow Brick transponder, which uses the Iridium satellite network to transmit the boat's position every four hours from anywhere on Earth. The race organisers therefore knew where we were and what our progress had been on a daily basis. Every two or three days we would speak to race control for one of our routine 'check-in, we are all still alive' calls. It was always a pleasure to speak to race officer Ian Couch who is an experienced ocean rower and therefore very aware of the conditions at sea. He was able to provide helpful information and advice and he was fully aware that the crews do go a bit mad after a month of rowing, so he would take whatever crazy thing we said to him with a smile. The content of the call was typically a check on the status of the boat and the health of the crew and a weather briefing. This was followed by a bit of a chat and update on our competitors' positions and status.

And then Ian said the magic words: 'You guys are on track for a world-record time...'

After all of our planning and training, all of our rowing efforts and all of the physical pain and mental exhaustion that we had been through to this point, it was just incredible to hear those ten words. We were five guys who had never rowed until two years previously but now we had a chance to become the fastest five-man crew ever to row across the Atlantic Ocean. We had dreamt of achieving the record, we had planned as if we could achieve the record and now our performance over the next ten days would decide whether we actually broke the record and became world champions.

In the space of ten seconds Ian had inspired us, re-energised us and reset our focus. Now we knew that we absolutely had to make our boat go as fast as possible until we landed in Antigua. Suddenly we were less tired!

Leaders in every role

All of the planning and preparation of the past three years had come down to this. What could we do as a crew to get the boat to go faster over the next ten days? Skipper Chris led a five-man discussion inviting ideas and suggestions. All thoughts were examined and debated.

Rowing absolutely flat out for the next 10 days would test our bodies and place our minds under greater stress than had been the case so far. Could we even do that? We needed to manage our situation before we became casualties of our own enthusiasm. We agreed that we needed to reallocate responsibilities and have leaders for each aspect of our performance: Chris would be responsible for weather routing, navigation and for making overall decisions. Will would act as the support to Chris, checking navigation and making course corrections while Chris slept. Sam would check performance and nutrition levels. Matt would monitor health, treat any injuries and maintain wellbeing. I would be responsible for boat engineering and maintenance.

All of these elements of performance needed to be monitored and optimised if we were not going to blow up our bodies or break the boat while chasing the world record.

Win as a team or lose as a team

By this stage we were 25 days into rowing flat out for two hours at a time with only the usual two-hour break to eat, sleep, toilet and recover. Our bodies were tired and while we had become familiar with the short sleep pattern, it was key to maintaining performance that the rest period was exactly that – complete rest. Allocating responsibilities meant that each of us could focus on our area and not expend physical or mental energy by worrying about or getting involved in the other tasks.

The objective of this planning was to get as much raw power through the oars as possible, for as much time as possible. We needed to maximise rowing and minimise distractions, which included necessary boat maintenance and management. After much discussion we agreed that two-man rowing was faster than three-man rowing. With three big guys rowing, we had found that the sweep of the oars for the forward-most rower was compromised. Depending on how lumpy the sea was, his back and arms could bump into the forward cabin and this would impact on his stroke rate and synchronisation. We agreed to trial a two-plus-two rowing schedule. This meant that we had one man spare. While we were all physically fit and had all trained hard for the race, Sam was a Team GB triathlete, Matt had competed in triathlon, boxing and other sports at university level and beyond, and Chris and Will were highly fit marine experienced athletes. They were also all half my age. So, it was agreed, the rowing pairs would be Chris with Matt and Will with Sam.

My role would be to provide total support to the rowers – as well as maintenance and communication. The maintenance included changing seat wheel bearings (we changed over 20 sets of bearings on the crossing), rebuilding foot straps, repairing the water maker, monitoring battery levels and checking the autohelm. Communication included calls to race control and to our families who were now planning the dates for their flights to Antigua. I needed to make sure that drinks, hot water and food were always available, the boat was clean and tidy, trash was stowed (all food packing would be counted at the end of the race and penalties applied if trash was lost overboard) and, perhaps most importantly, that the music player was working!

It would have been easy to feel disappointed that I wasn't rowing for the next few days but there was simply no room for pointless ego. The jobs all had to be done and as a team we had made our decision on the best way to achieve that while maximising rowing effort. We had worked hard to build a positive culture during our preparation for the race and now we needed to demonstrate real team spirit. That meant each of us proudly giving 120 per cent to whatever part we played in making the boat go faster.

11: NOTES FOR BUSINESS

Most people want to be good at what they do. Some people want to be very good. A few people are determined to do what it takes to be world class. In sport it is sometimes easy to determine who is the best since we can measure the fastest, highest or most wins. In business such distinction is less clear as we can measure success in dimensions including size, sales, profitability or customer satisfaction. Becoming world class in business is about more than the numbers. It is about providing a complete, positive and memorable experience for the client.

There is no easy solution to building a world-class organisation. Once you have a clear vision of what success will look like – and you are aware that the measure of success will change as the team or organisation develops – you have a starting point to build from. Planning will take you so far, but the real solution will emerge as a result of the experience of implementation and frequently through the mistakes that are made. There is the potential to make mistakes each time the organisation strives to deliver something beyond that which it is capable of. Each of these situations is a lesson for the business and an opportunity for the team to grow. Finding a way around the challenges encourages the team to develop a healthy disregard for the impossible. This is the mindset shift which is crucial to nudge the organisation towards world class.

Inspiring the team with the excitement of the journey and engaging them in the acceptance of missteps as a route to success builds a culture of determination and innovation. Each member of the team is invited to be accountable for the development of the organisation and encouraged to be ambitious in providing the best possible client experience each and every time.

Target world class
Someone somewhere is the best at what you are aiming to do. If you intend to build something extraordinary, they should be your guide. Why should you not be the best?

Recognise that there is only one version of the truth
Take a dispassionate look at your operation or team. Be thorough and honest. Identify weaknesses and look for opportunities for improvement. Identify strengths and areas that you can build on. This is the starting point. Share the analysis with your team and invite ownership.

There is no place for ego
Owning the challenge to become extraordinary is a team responsibility. Identifying areas for improvement is about critiquing the operation, not about criticising individuals. Seeking progress is an opportunity for everyone to grow and develop. There is no time to waste on massaging individual egos.

It won't work for everyone
As the team leader you are building towards your agreed version of success. This may not suit everyone in the team. Recognise and accept that some team members may choose not to come on the journey, or you judge that they will not make the step to be extraordinary. Be prepared to part as friends.

The difference is at the interface
A team leader cannot be everywhere in the organisation. The experience must be world class wherever the client touches the business in both the real and the virtual world. This requires the development of leaders who will set the example for the standard expected at every level in the organisation.

Demonstrate respect at all times

Everyone in the team has a critical role to play. There's no such person as 'only' a rower, or 'only' a team manager or 'only' a boat cleaner. Each team member must perform their role to an extraordinary level if the whole team is to be considered extraordinary. No matter what their position is, they influence overall performance. Be inclusive of everyone in the team.

12 ACHIEVING WORLD CLASS

You can get to world class. You can make excuses. You can't do both.

– Robin Sharma

We had ten days to deliver a world-class performance if we were to become the fastest five-man crew ever to row across the Atlantic. But we wanted to be absolutely certain about the timing for the new transatlantic record. We were operating across many time zones and our thinking needed to be clear. Exactly how many days and hours did we have? At what time did we have to arrive in Antigua – in Antiguan time?

We checked, checked and checked again. Will volunteered to record hours and miles rowed. Each day we set a target of miles we needed to cover if we were to succeed.

As each day counted down the clock seemed to move faster than the miles reduced.

Big results come from attention to small details

We had changed our shift pattern and rowed two-man teams. We reduced to zero the time spent by the rowers on support and maintenance. Physically we could not row any faster nor realistically further improve our rowing technique. We constantly examined the boat and ourselves to identify other ways to find more speed.

Precise navigation was key. Our brief to Stokey had been to guide us to the most direct, potentially most risky, route. If necessary, he would warn us on the daily weather briefing that we were heading into heavy seas but we asked Stokey to leave it to us to deal with the difficult conditions. We knew precisely what we would be facing because Stokey's forecasting was incredibly accurate. A couple of hours later as we were being bashed and crashed around, we did occasionally wonder whether we had chosen the best option but we had faith in Stokey and knew that the energy of the rougher water would be helping us to achieve the maximum speed towards the finish line.

The rowing pairs continued with the sprint sessions and competition over the distance covered in each two-hour shift. Anything above seven nautical miles per shift was a big motivator. We monitored our compass bearing and progress continuously, obsessively checking the VMC (velocity made good on course – in other words, the speed towards Antigua) and tweaking the autohelm to maximise the positive effect of the wind or current. Just a 0.1-knot improvement maintained over 10 days would be an increase of 24 nautical miles in distance covered, the equivalent of eight hours' rowing.

To further increase our speed, we looked at how we might be able to reduce the weight of the boat. Race regulations stipulated that we carry provisions for 55 days. That was 1,110 meals, 275 snack packs and 222 wet food emergency rations. In addition, we carried 50 litres of emergency drinking water. As we got closer to Antigua it was clear that we would not eat all of the food we had on board. Race rules dictated that, on penalty of disqualification, we could not touch the emergency wet rations or emergency drinking water. With now only seven or eight days' rowing left we still had almost half of the snack packs uneaten. Each one weighed at least one kilo. Keeping ten days' food supply (plus emergency rations) on board in case of any problems, we pooled resources, choosing the snacks we liked best and sharing the rest with the fish. Carefully unwrapping each snack and stowing the trash for scrutineering (and more importantly not littering the ocean) we lowered the weight of the boat by 30 or 40 kg. Another two per cent improvement!

Preparing for the finish

Our sprint tactics had worked. The change to the rowing rota, improved management of the boat and five days of extremely hard work had bought us time. With 370 miles left to row to Antigua, we had built a cushion of over 24 hours for our expected time of arrival (ETA) versus the previous world record. Everyone was tired but spirits were sky high as we returned to normal rowing rotas and enjoyed a kind break in the weather. We had entered the home straight with the famous trade winds and following rolling swells now driving us on.

Journal, January 14th 2020

Last 5 days have been hectic – everyone working so hard to make the boat go faster. The guys have been phenomenal and rowed so well. Morale is great but everyone is very, very tired. Changed bearings on more than 20 seat wheels, now out of replacements. Reusing damaged sets hoping they will last the course... watermaker stuttered but reset. Holding everything together for the finish...

We continued to check our ETA in Antiguan time to make sure that our calculations were correct. It would have been a tragedy to miss the record through an error in managing time zones. We still had four days' rowing at least and there was no room for loss of focus at this late stage. We accepted that we would not catch the first two boats, Fortitude IV and Rowed Less Travelled, but we were still closing in on BROAR who were 40 miles ahead. The DoraBros four-man team were 80 miles behind us. Barring a disaster, or a mistake in navigation, we did not believe they could catch us. Despite each of these boats being in a different race class to us, this close competition spurred us on to keep rowing, keep racing.

For the past week we had been liaising with race control and our families to coordinate their arrival in Antigua to welcome us at the finish. Holidays are precious and the plan was for the families to arrive shortly before we did to allow for the maximum time together in Antigua. Progress across the Atlantic in a rowing boat does not run to a predictable timetable. Over the past week our families had been reorganising their flights and hotel bookings daily as our projected finish time had moved back and forth. Since our families were travelling from the United Kingdom, we used Will's calculations and the weather forecast for the next three days and called the families to say that we believed we would hit land on 17 January. The families were a little bit surprised at the progress we had made with our sprint over the past five days, so now there was another race – would the families get to the finish line before us?

We were hoping to arrive at the finish line during daylight hours. Antigua is a beautiful island and the scenery around the finish line in English Harbour is stunning. The people of Antigua are wonderful supporters of the race and they turn up, along with hundreds of tourists, to welcome each arriving crew. We knew that if we arrived in daylight, we would cross the finish line cheered on by crowds standing on the walls of Fort Berkeley before gently rowing into Nelson's Dockyard, where the superyachts traditionally welcome transatlantic rowers with a symphony of air horns. It would be an amazing experience but we still had four days of hard rowing ahead of us to endure before we could begin to enjoy the arrival.

12: NOTES FOR BUSINESS

Achieving a world-class level of performance requires focus, determination and a lot of hard work. The difference between those people who achieve a superior level of performance and those who don't often comes down to just how much they want it. It is not about how successful you are; it is about how successful you want to be and then having the resolve to implement a plan to achieve it. There are plenty of reasons not to do that. Some people are happy to take the easy route to mediocrity. Other people want to be liked more than they want to be excellent and therefore never force change or push boundaries. Then there are those who never begin the journey because they are afraid of failure. While these reasons are valid excuses for not achieving what could be possible, accepting any of them means that you are prepared for your performance, or that of your organisation, never to reach world class.

Leaders who achieve world class are self selecting. They are determined and have to answer the question of just how much they and their team want it. If the answer to that question is not 100 per cent positive then you have team members who are unlikely to be inspired by the journey to world class. Team selection is a critical part of the process. Leaders must choose people who will walk, and will help others to walk, the journey to excellence and then support them to overcome the challenges and fears they will face on the way. Humans are not born with a fear of business failure. It is a learned condition which can be unlearned. A supportive and inspiring culture will encourage team members to focus on what can go right rather than worrying about what can go wrong. Teams will gain confidence in an environment where clear goals, effective communication, delegated trust, honest praise and reliable information form the basis of the operation. Achieving world class requires focus, agility and innovation. That is most effectively achieved when the team have factual information about the overall progress of the organisation and feel that they are directly involved in driving it forward.

Encouraging world-class performance is a continuous process. Organisations which are conventionally good will be overtaken by teams which continuously strive to be better. Innovation is the result of focused imagination. Fear of change can be further removed by the creation of a positive loop of advancement where execution results are reported back and identified areas of innovation are implemented. Successful ideas show progress; unsuccessful ideas are not an excuse to stop but instead are areas to reconsider, adapt and try again.

Seeking world class never ends

The process of development is perpetual. It involves the team continuously aiming beyond what it is currently capable of. As the organisation makes progress, the operating environment around it will change. Maintain momentum by evaluating market shifts and using data to accelerate your journey to world class.

Formally review your goals

Maintain a structured evaluation of the organisation's progress. Every 500 days conduct a complete review of the performance of the organisation and objectively evaluate progress. At this point redefine world class in view of environment dynamics. If necessary, adjust the long-term goals. Include team members in the discussion and support understanding by cascading the outcome fully through the organisation.

Leadership is not how much power you have, but how much you give away

Delegate responsibility for driving change to the team, ensuring everyone understands that they are provided with the authority to make changes and the accountability to be responsible for the required transformation. Leaders should not focus on being liked, rather on being respected. Driving change requires leaders to ensure clarity of communication and consistency of message.

Transformation to world class takes time

Except for the resolution of obvious issues, achieving a significant and sustainable improvement in operations and customer perception takes time. Work to a timescale of 1,000 days. Set ambitious targets for change but do not adopt shortcuts. World-class performance is built on a solid foundation of process and control.

Always look in the dark corners

Seek the areas of the organisation which are subject to minimal change and expose them. Continuously challenge processes and invite fresh thinking. Encourage the team by sponsoring each individual's growth and development. Consider carefully then make team changes where necessary.

Create agents of change

Each individual in the team should be the expert in their area of responsibility. Foster innovation and praise each example of fresh thinking which improves the organisation. Encourage the team to push boundaries and then get out of their way.

13 ANTIGUA AHOY!

It always seems impossible until it's done.

– Nelson Mandela

The first lights of Antigua came into sight just after dark on 16 January. After checking that we weren't seeing lights from a cargo vessel we cheered and then got back to work. It was a wonderful boost but we had eight hours of rowing ahead of us. We had not heard from our families and we weren't certain that they had arrived in Antigua for what we now knew, barring any surprises, would be a very quiet finish at about 3 am on 17 January. That would give us a 23-hour improvement on the previous record but we didn't know whether we would be celebrating alone. We briefly considered holding off at sea for a few hours to wait for daybreak and the traditional welcome party to form but quickly dismissed that idea. We were here to win a race and to set a new world record, not to keep people waiting so that our egos could be buffed by cheering crowds and air horns.

We had been warned that the approach to English Harbour was an area of dangerous rocks and tricky currents.

Apparently, if we missed the harbour entrance we could be swept along the south coast of Antigua by the prevailing wind and current and would find it very difficult to get back. Sleep was forgotten, concentration was critical and Chris checked and rechecked his navigation calculations.

We had been applying the mantra of 'look like a world-class team, perform like a world-class team' throughout our entire Ocean5 campaign. As we approached the finish, we discussed whether to change into our branded team kit, which had been carefully stowed after departure and was ready for our arrival. After 36 days at sea in hell, wind and big water we decided against it. We would arrive as we had rowed, each of us wearing shorts, safety harness, personal safety beacon and blisters! Any world-class reference would come from our finish time.

Good morning Antigua

The high-powered speedboat zoomed out of the darkness and took us by surprise. It was 3 am and the Atlantic Campaigns boat was suddenly alongside to escort us over the last half mile and make sure we didn't miss the entrance to the harbour. Having seen nobody except crewmates for the past 36 days it was a bit overwhelming to hear shouted greetings from the race officers, Atlantic Campaigns staff and various journalists on the official boat.

Their searchlights and TV lights beaming through the darkness were blinding and prevented us from seeing the finishing buoys at the entrance to the harbour. After some shouted instructions from the officials to 'go this way', 'no, that way', they said... 'That's it, you've crossed the finish line, you've done it!'

All was calm. We really had done it, crossing the finish line at 3.30 am. We had rowed across the Atlantic Ocean in 35 days, 19 hours, 50 minutes. That was 23 hours faster than the previous world record for a five-man crew.

With crew hugs and handshakes all around we lit flares and cheered as the official boat zipped around us with a camera crew recording the scene. Flares extinguished, we slowly rowed the final half mile to the quayside in Nelson's Boatyard. It was 3.45 am and all was quiet. We didn't pass cheering crowds, nor did we receive a jubilant symphony of air horns from the superyachts in the harbour, but that didn't matter. We enjoyed the quiet satisfaction of knowing we had set out to deliver a dream – and we had delivered it.

As we came around the superyachts, the quayside came into view. Now we could see our families and friends with the Atlantic Campaigns team, waving Ocean5 posters, flags and flares and cheering us in. They had made it ahead of us – just! Thankfully, they had landed in Antigua a few hours earlier and had headed directly to the finish area from the airport. We pulled up alongside the quay and stepped off Lady Jayne onto dry land for the first time in 36 days to realise that our legs didn't work. We had been living in a tiny moving platform for the past five weeks and our brains had become used to compensating. Now that we were on stationary ground, our vestibular system needed to adapt, which was going to take some time. That didn't matter because we didn't have to walk far.

We were surrounded by people and engulfed in hugs and congratulations from family and friends. In the midst of all of the commotion Sam proposed to his girlfriend (who delightfully accepted) and to cap it all off Atlantic Campaigns served burger, chips, Coke and beer... what a result! We were checked out by the medics who confirmed that between us we had lost 52 kg of body weight and our metabolic ages had reduced by an average of 12 years each. As the doctors happily diagnosed, we were fine. We knew we were fine although the hammering that we had taken during the past few weeks meant that every part of our body was aching, sore or blistered in one way or another. We also knew that these were superficial injuries and we would recover very quickly.

Atlantic Campaigns hosted a brief podium session of formal speeches and celebratory photographs and the official world-record time was confirmed. After some interviews with the press, that was it. Our adventure had reached its end. We had dared to dream, we had built our plan to achieve our goals, we had performed to the absolute best of our ability against that plan and we had broken the world record. And now it was all over.

Back to the real world

Leaving Lady Jayne in the care of the Atlantic Campaigns team we were ready to head to our hotels. Since all of the arrangements had been made by our families none of us had any idea where we were going. Splitting up with the crew as we each headed for a different hotel felt very odd. We had been within one metre of each other for almost 40 days and had come to rely on each other totally. It was strange to be separating and going back to our regular lives.

I finally got to bed, a real bed, at about 5.30 am. A warm shower was a wonderful luxury but the excitement and the complete change of environment meant that sleep didn't come easily. Even walking from the bathroom to the bed was a challenge as my legs refused to go where I pointed them and my body was sore all over.

Journal, January 17th 2020

That's it, all over and we did it. A NEW WORLD RECORD. Still coming to terms with what we have achieved. The team were amazing, the boat was great and we did what we set out to do. We faced some challenges but didn't have one argument in the entire crossing. Start as friends, finish as friends. So proud to be part of this team.

Following an amazing breakfast of fresh fruit and coffee, we were all back in the boatyard by midday to clean, unload and prepare Lady Jayne for her homeward journey. It was an oddly intimate exercise to unload her. We made mental notes about some of the equipment we had taken but never used – and would not take on another ocean crossing. We found that the locker holding our life raft was flooded with 30 or 40 litres of seawater, which was frustrating as it would have slowed us down and was something we would check for should we ever do another crossing. Mostly we found that personal kit and equipment which would normally last for years on land had taken a lifetime of wear and tear in only 36 days at sea. It reinforced to us, as if we needed the reinforcement, that we really had been operating in a brutal environment.

Lady Jayne would be packed into a shipping container and we would see her again in England in a few weeks' time. She had served us well and protected us from the ocean. We had grown very attached to her. She had been stable and steadfast even in the worst of conditions and she had kept us safe. It was a poignant moment as we finally walked away from her but we knew that both she and we would be going on to enjoy new adventures.

At anchor

Rowing an ocean is a completely immersive encounter with another world. It is an opportunity to experience incredible sights and sounds, to suffer extreme highs and terrifying lows and to build a team spirit of an intensity which is difficult to repeat. Once we had delivered the record, elation was mixed with relief. Extreme emotions take time to dissipate and after 36 days of constant anxiety it takes some time to relax. For me, there was a feeling of mild sadness that the adventure was over. I have taken part in many extreme expeditions and each has been an extraordinary life-enhancing experience. The ocean row had been, in a number of ways, more extreme than some of my previous adventures. Living in a tiny bubble with four other guys and looking out every day at the never-ending ocean created a bond within the team that is hard to compare. Enduring an Atlantic storm in a tiny plastic rowing boat and then turning that boat over in the middle of a vast ocean has given me exciting memories that will live with me forever. The knowledge that we survived those challenges and learned from them made us even stronger as a team. As William Arthur Ward said, 'Adversity causes some men to break; others to break records.' We hadn't broken.

For the first few days on shore, we each retreated to our families. After seven weeks of living in a shared bubble with our senses pummelled and overloaded, we each wanted space. We took some time to decompress from the incredible experience we had shared as we recovered physically and emotionally. We also needed to reconnect with our families and our normal lives, with the people who had been so generous in giving us the time and space to enter the race in the first place.

That quiet time gave us the chance to reflect; on the experience, on the lessons learned, on the enjoyment of being in the race and, above all, the opportunity of sharing it with a great team. In my case the extraordinary privilege of sharing the crossing with my son. We realised how grateful we were to our wider team, including my daughter Sara, who had driven the Ocean5 marketing efforts, and the amazing wives, girlfriends, parents, families and friends who had supported us with fundraising and activities. We were grateful that, despite their natural concerns for our safety, our families had never once tried to talk us out of entering the race.

We were thankful for our amazing sponsors who helped us to raise over $250,000 for the Plastic Soup Foundation and other organisations striving to protect the Earth's oceans.

We were hugely appreciative of the entire Atlantic Campaigns team for organising the race, creating the opportunity for us to enter and providing advice and support whenever we needed it.

We were indebted to Rannoch Adventure for building such a strong boat as Lady Jayne. She never let us down and she protected us in the most extreme conditions.

We extend our enormous respect to the great teams with incredible athletes who made it such a demanding race. We knew from the beginning that we could not out-row them, but we planned to be the best we could possibly be and we were determined that, once on the water, we would deliver everything we had.

And of course, I am more grateful than I know how to say to my incredible crewmates Chris, Matt, Sam and Will. We agreed that we would start the race as friends and finish as friends and that we would do everything we could to break the world record while still enjoying the crossing. We were four millennials and a boomer, and we made it work. We are still great friends; we had an amazing adventure and with the help of many people, we achieved each of our objectives.

The Ocean5 project successfully delivered.

Lady Jayne, out.

13: SUMMARY

Somebody always sets the standard. There is always a person, a team or an organisation which is the best of the best. I have called that standard world class. Achieving world class is extremely challenging, but as I have described in this book, if you are committed and follow a process, it is possible.

Some teams and businesses may appear to be effortlessly world class – but they are not. A lot of thought and effort has gone, and continues to go, into the design and delivery of each and every part of these organisations. I have led businesses where we improved our service level from 35 per cent to 85 per cent. I have also led businesses where we improved our service level from 92 per cent to 98 per cent. Leading the second of those businesses was a far greater challenge because it required fresh thinking and a significant revolution in our approach rather than an evolution of existing processes. Achieving world class requires a clarity of objective backed by a determination to succeed. It means examining and improving every single part of the organisation and driving substantial change where necessary. It requires thinking to be at a completely different level than was ever considered before. It requires honesty and the capacity to respect but reject previous operating standards.

A leader must first accept the responsibility for delivering world class and be able to display truthful authority on how it can be achieved. That does not mean having all of the answers but rather explaining why the goal is achievable and demonstrating trust in the team's ability to find the way to deliver it. The leader can then set the way and invite others to follow. Commitment to the goal and a shared belief in the team's capability to deliver it will build the driving force necessary for success.

To take that forward requires the responsibility for the implementation of the plan to be accepted by each member of the team. Creating an exciting and aspirational culture where ownership of the challenge is shared by everyone in the team is one of the most enjoyable aspects of leadership. A culture of personal responsibility, supporting a conviction that practical execution is everything, will drive the organisation to the next level. If the team continue on that journey, then a world-class level of performance becomes an achievable reality.

This is a process that I have been fortunate enough to lead numerous times in business. In those businesses we had fun while achieving results beyond what we ever expected. The Ocean5 project was different. We were not a business but a team of people who had chosen to set out to achieve a goal that most people thought was impossible. We were five novice rowers who shared a total commitment to the goal of a new world record and an absolute determination to deliver that goal. Within the Ocean5 crew our shared responsibility and culture of performance was so strong that project leadership by one individual was not necessary. We each took the lead when needed.

The principles that we applied will work in any situation and are shown below. They can be employed to demonstrate that the impossible is, in fact, doable.

- ➡ As a leader of yourself, your team, your division or your company, you must set the standard.
- ➡ Define what success will look like, sound like and feel like and why you need to achieve it.
- ➡ A clear plan of approach, carefully communicated, makes the impossible appear doable.
- ➡ Be very honest about the current level of performance of your team or organisation.
- ➡ Create an exciting culture where ordinary people can achieve extraordinary results.
- ➡ Remember, your team includes your colleagues, suppliers, partners and clients.

➡ Invite the team on a journey – engage their pride in creating world class.

➡ Encourage innovation, build momentum and drive change.

➡ Focus on execution and delivery; measure impacts.

➡ Communicate progress; celebrate each win.

➡ Enjoy the journey and stay positive.

14 THE VIEW FROM THE CREW

The strength of the team is each individual member. The strength of each member is the team.

– Phil Jackson

SAM COXON

When I was growing up my main sporting interest was dinghy racing. I started my working career as a member of superyacht crews and enjoyed a few years travelling the world's oceans before leaving to set up as a personal trainer. I had a call from a good friend, Will Hollingshead, who I had worked with on board yachts and he asked me whether I would be interested in rowing across the Atlantic. I had never thought of rowing an ocean, or even realised that it was something that people did. I was on a walking holiday with my mum when Will called so I discussed the invitation with her. She instantly said she thought it was a crazy idea and that I shouldn't go, but I decided it sounded like an amazing adventure that I just couldn't turn down!

We got together as a group and discussed the idea. We

agreed on the way it would work and as we set out our goals and objectives it was clear that we all wanted to be a competitive team. When we decided that we wanted to set the world record, I was in. While we were fully aware there was a huge amount of preparation to be done, I was so excited by the possibility. We created a plan which would get us to the start line, and then the finish line, in good shape. We knew that breaking the world record was going to be very challenging but we were determined to do everything we could to make it a reality.

My area of responsibility within the team was the fitness and training of the team members. I had to ensure that we were all capable of rowing across the Atlantic Ocean. This was an extreme challenge in many ways as the crew needed to have a high cardio fitness level and also be physically strong. We also needed to carry some body fat as we would be losing a lot of weight on the crossing so I didn't want the guys to train as if for a triathlon.

This type of marathon rowing is not something that has been done many times. I struggled to find available information on suitable training regimes. I researched online, through my fellow trainers and also spoke to a number of previous rowers. It became clear very quickly that strength training in the form of rowing-specific movements including deadlifts, rows, squats and core was the main area to work on. Core strength was very important as the crew would need to be robust and resilient enough to be able to stay upright and continue rowing despite frequent battering and bruising from the rough waves and heavy chop. We would also have to be flexible. With over two million rowing strokes expected, body flexibility and hands and forearm strength would need to be conditioned to simply hold on to the oars.

I developed a training plan which covered cardio and strength exercises. This included time on the rowing machine and real-life rowing when we were out on training weekends. We measured every training session that was completed and I set targets for each of the crew to achieve. For extreme events such as the row, mental preparation plays as much of a role as physical preparation. The training targets we set were designed to be very challenging, with obstacles set to increase the level of difficulty. This was intended to encourage each crew member to really push to their limit and build mental resilience for the race. I was delighted with the effort that everybody put into the training and we arrived in La Gomera in very good shape. Seven weeks later I was pleased and relieved that every one of the team made the crossing in one piece and arrived in Antigua with no significant injuries.

While the physical training schedule we worked to was very demanding, the most challenging part of the whole process for me was the fundraising. This was the first time that I had been involved in a sponsored event and I realised quickly that asking people for money was not my strong point. I could make my contribution to the team effort through my physical fitness but I struggled to paint as good a picture, or tell as passionate a story, as some of the other guys. I knew from my years of competitive triathlon experience that I had the fitness and strength to get through the training and the row, but I was concerned about whether we were going to raise enough money for our charity. In the end, the other guys used their skills to find generous sponsors and we were able to meet our target for funding the Plastic Soup Foundation.

After over two years of training, planning and organising, the build-up to the race in La Gomera was amazing. It was exciting to meet the other crews and to see how they had prepared themselves and their boats. The organisers, Atlantic Campaigns, were very thorough and the rules for entering the race were long and detailed. From an organisational perspective we felt we were in really good shape by the time we got to La Gomera. I felt very proud when we were told that our crew and boat were the best prepared in the fleet.

The race start was great fun and we got off to a fast start. I remember being pleased that we were making such good progress and that our rowing was going so well. We were moving forward through the fleet and reached second place overall. Then the weather turned for the worse. As we got out of the lee of the islands the strong wind and waves hit us and started to throw us all over the place. Then the storm hit us and it was like being in a washing machine. The oars snapped and I remember that we were all shocked by the force of the water. I was rowing at 4 am; it was very cold and very dark; waves were coming at us from every direction and constantly breaking over the boat. We were fighting just to keep the boat moving forwards and not get swamped or capsized in the heaving sea. Honestly, I was terrified – in fact, I think that we all were but we didn't have time to waste thinking about it. I was so impressed by how we worked as a team through that storm – we never gave up fighting and there wasn't one word of complaint.

I found the early part of the race to be the most difficult and uncomfortable. For the first two or three days after the storm the weather was very bad. We had food stored in our forward cabin because there was too much of it to fit into the food lockers. Matt, Will and I were sharing a small cabin and space was extremely limited. During the rough weather we were sleeping in wet foul weather gear, in case we were suddenly needed on deck. This made sleeping very difficult and we never got more than 60 or 70 minutes of sleep between shifts. I remember that each time the cabin door opened I would get a spray of salt water over my face just as I was dreaming of being at home in my lovely bed! It didn't help that I was also suffering from acute seasickness.

Living on board such a small boat was tough. Five big blokes need a lot of room but there wasn't any. We had to learn to live within the confines of the boat. Having worked on boats in the past and lived in close quarters I know what it's like to be confined to a small space, but living on an eight-metre-long boat (where four metres is taken up by rowing seats) with four other guys is taking it to a whole new level! There is no room, or time, for untidy kit so we learned to accept the limitations of the space and always show respect to our crewmates. That included the night of the storm when the only space to grab a few minutes' sleep was lying spooned with Matt, both of us soaking wet and in full foul weather gear, in a cabin just about big enough for one of us. Over the first few days we managed to settle into the boat and we got clever at using every bit of space. As the routine improved, I enjoyed the quietness and simplicity of the race itself. Get up, row, clean, eat, row, sleep, repeat. There were no phones, emails or other communication. Except for calls to race control and Stokey, our weatherman, there was pretty much no outside contact.

This crossing taught me to appreciate just how important teamwork is, how to deal with situations calmly, how much the human body can take, how it is possible to function on minimal sleep, that it is not over until it is over and to NEVER give up. You have to trust your teammates in every situation. If they say jump, they are saying it for a reason and so you jump! We were a great team and the banter was fantastic. We sang songs and we told funny stories, full-frontal nudity and toilet comedy were just part of the trip – it is really tricky to sit on a toilet bucket which is sliding around a slippery deck as the waves wash over you! We learned to embrace every day as it comes and recognised that, since life is short, we should make the most of every situation and enjoy it all. Despite the tough conditions, we laughed our way across at least half of the Atlantic. In the middle of the ocean, 1,500 miles from any land, you have the chance to find your true self and what you really stand for. It was here I knew this was what I was meant to do – I was in my element.

The environment and seascape were awesome. The sunrises and sunsets were simply amazing; the stars and the moonlit skies were beautiful and I will remember seeing a moon rainbow for the rest of my life. I enjoyed looking out for the wildlife including whales and dolphins and dodging the flying fish as they glided over the boat. We had good days where we covered 90–100 miles with a strong tailwind and we had bad days where we covered fewer than 30 miles. Rowing as hard as we could into a headwind and only covering two miles in ten hours was soul destroying but the tunes stayed on, the spirits stayed high and we knew that every mile closer to Antigua meant that we were a mile closer to getting off the boat, seeing our families and enjoying our first pina colada! I have vivid memories of the capsize and how frightening it was to be knocked out of the boat by the huge waves which turned the boat over. But this had to be compared to the good days when we were enjoying every second of surfing down waves, music blasting through our speakers, loving life and looking forward to Antigua. We did get bashed about and everybody was hurting and more exhausted as each day passed, but we all kept going. There was never a cross word spoken, and we were all doing our bit to get to that finish line!

Crossing the finish line was amazing. I don't think any of us could quite believe that we had broken the record by 23 hours. It was such a wonderful experience as we pulled alongside the dock where our families were with their banners, signs, drums and flares. I just wanted to get off the boat to give everyone a hug.

I had prepared to propose to my girlfriend Tash when we arrived and this was one of the positive thoughts that kept me going during the tough times on the trip. I stepped off the boat and my sea legs wobbled all over the place before I dropped down on one knee and asked her to be my wife. I'm delighted to say that she said yes.

What a fantastic way to end an amazing adventure!

MATT GASKELL

I have partnered Kev on a number of expeditions and we had frequently discussed the Atlantic row but I didn't think he was serious about it. Then suddenly he was. By the time he spoke to me he had already met Will, Chris and Sam and it looked like it was going to happen. I was delighted as expeditions are what I like to do for fun and it is so much easier to organise something of this scale when you are part of a team and can share the workload. It was also excellent timing for me because I had just graduated in medicine and then, after a lot of thought, changed my career path. It had been a tough year and I wanted a big new project to look forward to.

Most people focus purely on the race itself, but I knew from my previous expedition experience that to be successful, the planning and preparation is at least as important as the expedition itself. For the Atlantic row I enjoyed the build-up phase; researching and choosing the boat, specifying the equipment, liaising with Rannoch during the construction phase and testing the equipment as it was fitted. I also enjoyed negotiating with suppliers for the food and medical supplies. I liked the fact that we were serious about our attempt to break the world record. That meant we had to be fully professional in every aspect of the preparation. It was our intention to be the best-prepared boat in the fleet.

My areas of responsibility during the preparation phase covered administration and rules compliance, medical support and boat quartermaster. I needed to conduct proper research and care in each of these areas was necessary to make sure we could eventually focus on the row itself. The rules for the race are very stringent and we would have to pass two stages of scrutineering; the second one would be in La Gomera and we had to make sure that we complied fully with each of the hundreds of stipulations. If we got to La Gomera with a non-compliance issue we could be excluded from the race. We knew that if we left it to everybody to read the rules, then nobody would. One of my jobs was to be the rules geek – to read the hundreds of pages of rules and make sure we complied in every way. It was a bit boring but absolutely necessary.

It was great to be doing an expedition with a new group of people. I had not met Will, Chris or Sam before but it was immediately clear that they were really good guys – they were also fit, strong and experienced at sea. It was enjoyable getting to know them and training with them. I was initially a bit concerned about whether I had the skills to cope with the crossing but we quickly learned to work well as a team and throughout the preparation stages I was excited about sharing the crossing with them. I liked the philosophy that we adopted on the boat – be kind – because we knew we were going to have some very difficult days on the crossing and we all had to support each other.

Since I have a medical degree, it was inevitable that I would be designated boat medic. That was fine as expedition medicine is a discipline that I enjoy. It was very challenging to pull together a medical kit which would be suitable for everything from a heart attack (Kev isn't a spring chicken any more although he thinks he is!), major blood loss (we used very sharp knives on the boat) or blunt trauma (someone being knocked out in a storm), to less urgent situations involving blisters and seasickness, while keeping the kit as compact and light as possible. I think we ended up with a suitable range of equipment and medicines but thankfully most of it was not tested during the row.

Since I was nominated to be responsible for the health

and wellbeing of the team, I had explored the experiences of previous teams and the medical issues that they had faced. I found that some previous teams had failed because a rower had suffered from agoraphobia (fear of being in open spaces or situations from where escape might be difficult) or thalassophobia (fear of the vastness and depth of the sea). I was concerned whether this may be an issue for us – probably not for the experienced mariners, but for Kev and me. Later, when we set to sea, I realised that being extremely low on the water meant the horizon appeared to be very close and, strangely, I never felt like we were actually that far from land.

Of course, everything that we were to take on the row had to fit into the boat and there really was very little space. It is always easy to add another piece of kit or a spare widget in case the first widget breaks. On previous expeditions I have seen people taking all kinds of luxuries and then regretting their decision after carrying their kit for a few days. I volunteered for the role of boat quartermaster – aka boat guard! Challenging every luxury or non-essential item (and some which were initially considered essential) is never a popular role but someone had to do it. We left behind a lot of weight and some luxuries and spare equipment. I was relieved that, during the row, we never once needed something which wasn't on the boat.

The start of the race was exciting and the first day was enjoyable but it all went wrong very quickly. The first night was bad. The speed at which the storm arrived was a complete surprise. Being in the middle of an Atlantic storm was a pretty disorientating experience. The wind and waves hammered the boat and the crew and we felt like we were fighting just to stay in control. Enormous waves swept over us and seemed to come from every direction. I was rowing when I saw Chris's oar break and I remember being shocked by the power of the water. Then the oar in my hand just went light and I realised that it had also snapped. With two of the oars broken, the boat was out of control for a while. The autohelm alarm was screaming and we had a difficult few hours keeping the boat stable and moving forwards so that the water didn't break any more kit – or us. I remember it being very cold and very intimidating. We fought to replace the broken oars with our two spares, which were lashed to the deck, and tried to keep rowing while the huge waves kept crashing over us. At that moment I felt that we really didn't have the experience to handle this situation (who does?) and for a while I was a bit worried. For the rest of that night, I was hugely impressed with Chris, Will and Sam who dug in and used their marine experience to keep Lady Jayne moving through the storm.

Healthwise we mainly experienced short-term issues; strangely the three mariners were badly seasick but that passed after a few days. We found that wearing foul weather gear when rowing caused injuries where the skin was rubbed off, causing blisters and infection, so we mostly gave up on the waterproofs and just got wet. Because of everything that was going on and the pounding that the boat was taking, there were times when we just didn't get any sleep. I don't believe that I slept at all for the first two days and nights after the storm. We were rotating three people in a two-person cabin every 60 minutes and it was impossible to get to sleep with the boat lurching around and the crew changes going on.

Once we were through the storm, we found our rhythm and I thoroughly enjoyed rowing on the warm sunny days. It was a bit less fun on a cold rainy night. Our rowing steadily improved as we got used to the way that the wind and the waves affected the boat. We worked well as a team with everyone pulling hard to get the best boat speed possible. I was pleased that the ration pack food I had recommended to the guys was tasty and popular. Eating a good warm meal quickly became a highlight of our day. The hot meals combined with the snack packs we had carefully created to include chocolate, nuts, cake, protein bars and anything else we fancied with a high calorific value, meant that we ate well. This was very important if we were to maintain our rowing power. As we became more familiar with the boat and the ocean we relaxed into the cycle of row, eat, wash, sleep, repeat, and learned how to get to sleep quickly once we came off the row shift. Again, this was critical to our overall health and performance but I do remember that falling into a deep sleep just made the wake-up call 80 minutes later all the more painful.

There were many routine tasks that needed to be done as well as the rowing. Each day we needed to perform various maintenance activities on the boat, run the water maker to make drinking water, distribute the drinking water around to all of the water bottles, heat water for food and occasionally get into the sea to clean the muck off the hull. I did feel a bit sorry for Chris and Kev in the aft cabin when they were caught by a rogue wave as they opened the cabin door. It wet everything in their cabin and they slept on sodden mattresses for much of the crossing.

Overall, it was a wonderful experience. The constantly changing ocean, the beautiful sky both during the day and at night and the wildlife which we saw made it very interesting. The skills within the team were very complementary and except for the excitement of the capsize I think we managed the boat well. We became great friends who had been tested under the most extreme of conditions. One of the biggest lessons I learned from the entire project was just how little kit we really needed. If you are resourceful then you can always find a way to fix or replace a lost part – make do and mend! Next time I take part in a similar expedition I will make sure we take even less.

Setting a new world record changed the way that I looked back on the row. It was a huge achievement and I was very proud to be part of the crew. When we had finished, I said that I would never row an ocean again. I soon altered that to saying I would never row the Atlantic again, but I would possibly row a different ocean. I have relaxed that again and am now working towards a row across the Pacific. The prospect of setting another world record is pretty compelling.

CHRIS HODGSON

Will Hollingshead called me and told me that he had entered me into a transatlantic rowing race. At first, I thought he was joking. But I was intrigued and agreed to meet the other guys and see how the conversation developed. Once we had discussed the challenge I was hooked. I grew up sailing dinghies and playing on water and my career as a superyacht officer means that I am comfortable being at sea, but this race was going to be the most physically demanding event that I had ever been involved with.

Before we ever got anywhere near the water, the preparation itself was a major commitment. We were a team of five people with busy schedules, some of whom lived and worked abroad. This made team calls, meetings and training sessions difficult to organise and carry out. Everyone had to be somewhat flexible and there were times when not all team members could make certain meetings or training sessions. We dealt with that as just another challenge to be overcome.

We also had to find sponsorship. I hadn't realised what a tough and time-consuming activity this was. We had decided to raise money to fight plastics in the oceans. Protecting the seas was something that we were all passionate about. It was an advantage when approaching sponsors to be a team of five as a larger team meant we were each able to pursue more leads. Having not been involved with fundraising before, I was shocked at just how much work and persistence is required to secure any amount of money. Most companies and people I spoke with were very interested in what we were doing and expressed their interest to contribute but when it came to the crunch (cheque-writing time), things often went very quiet. We were very lucky to have Kev on our team, who through a long and successful career had made many great business contacts. It was through these connections that we were able to achieve our sponsorship goals and donate a considerable amount of money to our chosen charity, the Plastic Soup Foundation.

Immediately before the race started, I remember the anticipation, the excitement and the feeling that we had been building up to this moment for two and a half years. Radio interviews, TV, cameras, people on the dock waving and smiling. Then we were off.

As the skipper of Lady Jayne, I felt a great responsibility for the safety and wellbeing of the crew. Having been in roles of responsibility in a professional capacity, I was able to draw from experience and knew that preparation was going to be key. I would run through emergency situations in my head and think about how we could reduce the chances of them happening and what we'd do if they did. This was all good in theory but having never experienced an ocean row, I was reminded every day to stay humble as the ocean found a different way to demonstrate the dangers we were facing.

I will never forget the first night out from La Gomera. We found ourselves in the middle of a raging storm. As night fell, the waves got bigger and bigger. Trying to maintain our intended course meant that we were beam on to the waves. One rogue wave caused us to surf sideways down the wave and the two oars on the lower side got pinned against the boat. The force of the wave and the weight of the boat snapped my oar instantly; the next wave broke a second oar that Matt was pulling. We were just hours into the race and with a broken set of essential equipment. This coupled with extreme seasickness made for one hell of a night. But, after a few scary hours, we got through it.

One of the most vivid and happy memories of the row was surfing down the waves. Watching the waves build as they came towards us, wondering whether they were going to crash over us or pick us up. Then feeling the acceleration as we were lifted and sent surfing down the wave with pure exhilaration. After days and weeks of back-breaking rowing, the occasional feeling of the boat becoming totally weightless was just wonderful.

Despite the tough conditions we were a great team and we had a lot of fun. I will never forget everyone singing together on deck when we were alone in the middle of the ocean. The camaraderie we shared was wonderful. We had an amazing feeling of freedom knowing that there was nowhere else that we needed to be. We were exactly where we were supposed to be at that moment and nothing else mattered. Swimming naked in the middle of the crystal-clear ocean in water 5,000 metres deep was an extraordinary experience. We had to do it to clean the bottom of the boat but we kept looking down and wondering what predatory lifeform was looking back at us.

New Year's Eve was a wonderful day because we celebrated Christmas and New Year together. We stopped rowing for a while, and the sea gently rocked us as we watched the sunset, read letters and opened presents from loved ones at home while we shared the obligatory Terry's Christmas Chocolate Orange. It was a well-deserved rest from the oars and just a wonderful half an hour among a group of friends in an extraordinary location.

The highs of the row can't be truly appreciated without the low moments. Rowing for 12 hours every day was pretty tough but if people ask me what the worst thing about the row was, I always say 'Imagine sleeping on a sopping wet, salty mattress for 36 days.' Temperature variations were quite extreme. At night we could get very cold but the cabin had absolutely no insulation and in strong sunlight was unbearably hot with condensation dripping from the ceiling.

The boat was great and we felt very secure with her but she was forever being bounced around by big waves. I remember being in the cabin and scalding myself with boiling water while trying to make a meal. I had just come off the oars and was feeling particularly tired and hungry and just wanted to eat as fast as possible to maximise rest time. As I poured boiling water into the food pouch to rehydrate the meal, a wave struck the side of the boat causing me to spill boiling hot chilli con carne all over my leg. Not only was it extremely painful but the mess was unbelievable. I remember feeling angry, tired, helpless – and hungry!

One lesson I have taken from the row is how to deal with confrontation. When you are in a tiny rowing boat in the middle of the ocean there is no space to hide anything. It is a stressful environment, emotions run high and there is bound to be some friction. We handled any disagreement in an honest fashion, dealt with it swiftly and moved on without resentment. Before we started the row, we agreed to be kind to one another. Being in the middle of the ocean with four other people makes you realise that out there, at that moment in time, the other four people are the only people that matter. The relationships between us would make or break the experience.

Throughout the row, there was a never-ending roller coaster of emotions. Some of the humorous highlights still make me chuckle. Full frontal male nudity in every direction, watching teammates trying to balance on a bucket to do their business while the boat rolled violently in rough seas and the gibberish spoken by the crew while hallucinating due to sleep deprivation.

We learned to communicate effectively. In a normal

situation people can waste time and experience emotional hardship due to a lack of communication. We were not in a normal situation and did not have the space or time for poor communication. As much as we may like to think we are all excellent mind readers, we really are not. On the boat we talked issues out openly and quickly. In the middle of the ocean, honesty and trust between the crew are critical. It was a very intense environment and sometimes each of us needed some space. We learned that just saying 'I'm not in the mood for talking right now' is positive communication. We found that having a moment to yourself, and letting the others know that you wanted that space, was very helpful.

One of the biggest lessons I learned from the row was that you only live once! People say it all the time but mostly don't normally act in a manner that is aligned with the statement. It would have been very easy not to take on a challenge like this. Doubts and concerns pop up everywhere. Can I afford to take the time off work? Is it too risky or dangerous? Am I being selfish? Am I strong enough? Are we going to get on well as a team? Is it going to be as fun as we're imagining? From my experience, anything that is worth doing always carries some risks and concerns. I believe that when opportunities that make you excited present themselves, listen to your heart and follow it. Yes, there will be challenges to overcome, logistics to work out and sacrifices to be made, but without these difficulties, it would not be such a meaningful experience.

After taking part in the row, my advice to anyone considering a challenge of such a magnitude is to just go for it! Have the courage to take on the unknown. You will come out stronger and wiser. I believe that we should commit to living our life to the full, then build a plan and follow it. As the saying goes, life really does begin at the edge of your comfort zone. It is here that we are challenged. It is during these challenging encounters that we learn the most about ourselves, we grow, we gain new skills and we experience emotions never felt before. It is these challenges and how we react to them that build our confidence and knowledge.

The row was, without doubt, the most incredible experience of my life. It was the hardest, the most exciting, the happiest and the scariest thing I have ever done.

I truly cannot wait for the next adventure.

WILL HOLLINGSHEAD

Being involved in this row was a lucky case of being in the right place at the right time. I was living in the south of France through the summer and was a member of the Young Professionals in Yachting organisation. The YPY hosts seminars with talks by industry leaders who help to encourage professional development. At one of their events Kev gave a presentation on his business life and how he has used his experiences from various expeditions to establish a positive culture within the businesses he has led.

I really enjoyed the presentation and was inspired by his accounts of walking to the poles and climbing some of the world's biggest mountains. At the end of the presentation the audience were invited to ask questions. One of the questions asked was 'Mr Gaskell, you've done all these cool adventures and you've been successful in business – what would you like to do next?', to which Kev thought for a moment and then answered, 'I've always wanted to row the Atlantic but I've never found anyone daft enough to come with me. Would anyone here like to join me?'

Nobody took him seriously but it was a lightbulb moment for me. I realised that Kev had been talking about ordinary people doing extraordinary things and here I was possibly being invited to be involved in an amazing adventure. After the presentation, I approached Kev and we had a chat about the content of his talk and his idea of entering a team into the transatlantic rowing race. He admitted that it was an outrageous idea and he didn't, at that stage, have any firm plans to follow through. We exchanged details and agreed to stay in touch. Fast forward a couple of months and I was back in the UK. My work project in France had finished and I had some time on my hands. I had never stopped thinking about the possibility of the Atlantic row and how it could become a reality. I reached out to Kev on LinkedIn with the following message:

'Good afternoon, Mr Gaskell. We met at the YPY event at Monaco Yacht Club. Just a quick message to see if you're still interested in rowing across the Atlantic. I've been thinking about it for the last few months and it's a challenge I would love to take on. There are two other lads interested who are both ex yacht crew members. One of the guys is an Ironman athlete and the other is a personal trainer and CrossFit competitor. The idea would be to take part in the 2018 Atlantic Rowing Race and to do the whole thing for an ocean plastic clean-up charity. It would be great to hear your thoughts and understand if this is something you'd like to be involved in. Regards, Will Hollingshead'

Kev replied to me positively 30 minutes later and I realised that he was still keen. I knew that I should probably now mention it to Chris and Sam and see whether they were even interested in such an adventure. I had put them forward to be involved in the row without actually asking them!

We all met to discuss the idea over coffee. Kev's son Matt was keen to be involved and we soon realised that not only did we have a potentially competitive crew of five driven and focused individuals, but we also meshed very well as a team. In the type of stressful situations which the Atlantic row would present, combined with living in close quarters for weeks on end, a positive team spirit would be crucial to a successful and enjoyable crossing.

The preparation and the training were long, detailed and arduous. We shared the preparation responsibilities according to our skills and experience. One of my tasks was organising and managing the weekend-based training sessions in the Solent. This included planning around weather and tides, checking for any warnings from Southampton Port and making sure we had clearance from Lymington Harbour Authority to launch on their slip. The Solent and Southampton Water is one of the world's busiest shipping areas and is heavily populated by both commercial marine traffic and pleasure craft. We needed to plan our training rows to head for the quieter parts of the water while at all times keeping a very careful lookout for the tankers, naval ships, container ships and passenger cruise liners which may not see us. We had to be especially cautious near the ferry routes as those vessels were large and fast and ploughed day and night between Southampton and the Isle of Wight – and they stopped for nothing. We were a very small and slow vessel with an even smaller radar signature. AIS was no use in this area as there was always other traffic within a mile or two and so the alarm would go off all of the time if we switched it on. It was a good area to learn navigation and how to watch out for dangerous traffic.

We did pretty well and stayed out of trouble for most of our 18 months of training except for one entertaining and potentially dangerous episode when we were off Cowes entrance. I made an error of judgement when steering our boat out of the way of a 300-metre-plus car carrier. I had failed to anticipate that the carrier was about to swing to starboard and head for Southampton Docks. Instead of moving into clear water I had mistakenly steered us straight into the path of the approaching monster, which would not have even noticed as it cruised serenely over Lady Jayne. Thankfully someone else was watching and it all got a bit noisy when the harbour pilot arrived at full speed in his patrol launch with blue flashing lights and blaring siren. We were told, in no uncertain terms, what he thought about my navigation skills as we frantically turned and rowed out of the way. It was a mistake that we never intended to repeat but it taught us that our decision making when rowing and tired could become impaired. We needed to make sure that the effort of pulling each rowing stroke and a lack of sleep would not distract us from concentrating on everything else that we needed to do to make sure that Lady Jayne was both fast and safe.

When we got to La Gomera we were in really good shape and felt confident that we would be able to complete the Atlantic crossing well. Our time in final preparation was fun as we had formed into a really good and positive team. Our families arrived to spend a few days with us before the start of the race and that helped to calm any nervousness. In terms of the row itself, memories become hazy because we were frequently operating under conditions of high stress and low sleep. What I do remember is that we had a lot of fun and we also had some very difficult days.

My memories are centred on the lowlights of the most difficult and painful days and the highlights of the most amazing days and the sights we saw. The encounter with the terrific storm on our first night at sea is something that will stay with me forever. As an experienced mariner I have seen storms at sea before but being in such a tiny craft and feeling so vulnerable as we were thrown around by the wind and waves was a very scary experience. I think that for the entire crew it was only in the days after the storm that we fully realised just how dangerous the situation had been.

One of my most vivid memories is of the 20-hour period when we rowed into a strong headwind. This is probably the toughest weather condition for an ocean rowing boat. It makes the oars feel as if you are pulling them through thick treacle. If conditions worsen further, you may have to give up rowing and deploy the para anchor to reduce the rate of backwards drift.

We were a highly competitive bunch and we were chasing a world record. We decided that if we were able to make even the slightest headway into the wind, we would accept the pain and strain and keep rowing rather than sitting on the para anchor and slowly drifting back the way we'd come. In my 33 years on this planet those 20 hours spent rowing into that headwind are the hardest physically and mentally that I have ever endured. I have been challenged before, but two hours of flat-out rowing covering maybe 800 metres, knowing that you have to come back on the oars for another two hours after your brief rest, was a real test. I was so proud of the crew. In those 20 hours I didn't hear one single complaint. Each rower sucked up the pain and kept going, again and again.

The other memory which I will treasure is seeing a moonbow early one morning while rowing with Kev. The moonbow was created by the light of a full moon during a rain shower. It really was an amazing sight.

I've thought a lot about meeting Kev in Monaco and later following up to ask whether he was serious about the row. The whole experience was such a great learning opportunity and I am so pleased that I followed my instinct and sent that message. There are many people in this world who want to do great things and there are also people who have achieved great things but I learned from this experience that you won't get anywhere if you don't have an ambition, pluck up the courage to ask the question and then follow the opportunity that the question creates.

For the rest of my life if there is a business I want to start, or an adventure I want to pursue, then I will not hesitate to contact people like Kev and invite them to get involved. The worst that can happen is that they say no, in which case you have to look for another mentor. Of course, they may just say yes and then you end up as a member of a five-man team who enjoyed the adventure of a lifetime and set a new world record.

THE NUMBERS

Start: 12 December 2019, 11.40 am	San Sebastián de La Gomera, Spain
Finish: 17 January 2020, 03.30 am	English Harbour, Antigua & Barbuda
Crossing time	35 days, 19 hours, 50 minutes
Beat previous record by	23 hours
Total distance rowed	2,671 nautical miles/3,071 land miles (31 nautical miles shorter than the next shortest crossing, 1.1% distance saved)
Rowing strokes	Average stroke rate 20 per minute
	Total strokes by crew circa 2,500,000
Calorie burn	Average 7,000 per rower per day. Total 1,260,000 calories
Fitness	Team lost 52 kg in body weight.
	Average body fat below 8% at finish
	Metabolic age reduced by average of 12 years per rower
Training	Team rowed 4,800 km on static rowers
	Ran 4,400 km
	Cycled 9,250 km
	Lifted 2,248,938 kg (weight of a Royal Navy Frigate)

If there were no difficulties, there would be no successes. If there was nothing to struggle for, there would be nothing to be achieved.

– Samuel Smiles